Rock Climbing
Yosemite's Select

WARNING: CLIMBING IS A SPORT WHERE YOU MAY BE SERIOUSLY INJURED OR DIE.
READ THIS BEFORE YOU USE THIS BOOK.

This guidebook is a compilation of unverified information gathered from many different climbers. The author cannot assure the accuracy of any of the information in this book, including the topos and route descriptions, the difficulty ratings, and the protection ratings. These may be incorrect or misleading and it is impossible for any one author to climb all the routes to confirm the information about each route. Also, ratings of climbing difficulty and danger are always subjective and depend on the physical characteristics (for example, height), experience, technical ability, confidence and physical fitness of the climber who supplied the rating. Additionally, climbers who achieve first ascents sometimes underrate the difficulty or danger of the climbing route out of fear of being ridiculed if a climb is later down-rated by subsequent ascents. Therefore, be warned that you must exercise your own judgment on where a climbing route goes, its difficulty and your ability to safely protect yourself from the risks of rock climbing. Examples of some of these risks are: falling due to technical difficulty or due to natural hazards such as holds breaking, falling rock, climbing equipment dropped by other climbers, hazards of weather and lightning, your own equipment failure, and failure or absence of fixed protection.

You should not depend on any information gleaned from this book for your personal safety; your safety depends on your own good judgment, based on experience and a realistic assessment of your climbing ability. If you have any doubt as to your ability to safely climb a route described in this book, do not attempt it.

The following are some ways to make your use of this book safer:

1. **CONSULTATION:** You should consult with other climbers about the difficulty and danger of a particular climb prior to attempting it. Most local climbers are glad to give advice on routes in their area and we suggest that you contact locals to confirm ratings and safety of particular routes and to obtain first-hand information about a route chosen from this book.

2. **INSTRUCTION:** Most climbing areas have local climbing instructors and guides available. We recommend that you engage an instructor or guide to learn safety techniques and to become familiar with the routes and hazards of the areas described in this book. Even after you are proficient in climbing safely, occasional use of a guide is a safe way to raise your climbing standard and learn advanced techniques.

3. **FIXED PROTECTION:** Many of the routes in this book use bolts and pitons which are permanently placed in the rock. Because of variances in the manner of placement, weathering, metal fatigue, the quality of the metal used, and many other factors, these fixed protection pieces should always be considered suspect and should always be backed up by equipment that you place yourself. Never depend for your safety on a single piece of fixed protection because you never can tell whether it will hold weight, and in some cases, fixed protection may have been removed or is now absent.

Be aware of the following specific potential hazards which could arise in using this book:

1. **MISDESCRIPTIONS OF ROUTES:** If you climb a route and you have a doubt as to where the route may go, you should not go on unless you are sure that you can go that way safely. Route descriptions and topos in this book may be inaccurate or misleading.

2. **INCORRECT DIFFICULTY RATING:** A route may, in fact, be more difficult than the rating indicates. Do not be lulled into a false sense of security by the difficulty rating.

3. **INCORRECT PROTECTION RATING:** If you climb a route and you are unable to arrange adequate protection from the risk of falling through the use of fixed pitons or bolts and by placing your own protection devices, do not assume that there is adequate protection available higher just because the route protection rating indicates the route is not an "X" or an "R" rating. Every route is potentially an "X" (a fall may be deadly), due to the inherent hazards of climbing – including, for example, failure or absence of fixed protection, your own equipment's failure, or improper use of climbing equipment.

THERE ARE NO WARRANTIES, WHETHER EXPRESS OR IMPLIED, THAT THIS GUIDEBOOK IS ACCURATE OR THAT THE INFORMATION CONTAINED IN IT IS RELIABLE. THERE ARE NO WARRANTIES OF FITNESS FOR A PARTICULAR PURPOSE OR THAT THIS GUIDE IS MERCHANTABLE. YOUR USE OF THIS BOOK INDICATES YOUR ASSUMPTION OF THE RISK THAT IT MAY CONTAIN ERRORS AND IS AN ACKNOWLEDGEMENT OF YOUR OWN SOLE RESPONSIBILITY FOR YOUR CLIMBING SAFETY.

Compiled by
Don Reid

Rock Climbing
Yosemite's Select

CHOCKSTONE

FALCON®

Helena, Montana

DEVELOPED BY
Chockstone Press

Falcon Press Publishing Co., Inc.
PO Box 1718
Helena, Montana 59624

FRONT COVER
Johnny Dawes on Alien, The Rostrum north face. Photo by Matt Gray.
All uncredited photos by George Meyers.

Library of Congress Cataloging-in-Publication Data

Reid, Don.
    Rock climbing Yosemite's select / compiled by Don Reid. -- 2nd ed.
        p.   cm.
    Includes index.
    ISBN 1-57540-115-0
    1. Rock climbing--California--Yosemite Valley--Guidebooks.
  2. Yosemite Valley (Calif.)--Guidebooks.   I. Title
  GV199.42.C22Y67617   1998
  796.52'23'09794447---dc21   98-17872
                                                                        CIP

Acknowledgments

This book, for the most part, represents a digest of works preceding it. It would not
have been possible without the accumulated knowledge and efforts of those who have
documented climbing in Yosemite and served as an historical link. It all begins with a
grassroots accounting of climbing adventures and culminates in written guides.

First, my thanks go to Steve Roper and George Meyers for their monumental dedication
and skill in compiling previous editions of *Climbers Guide to Yosemite Valley* and *Yosemite
Climbs,* respectively. My gratitude is expressed as well to a long list of individuals who, in
different ways, have furnished contributions to this book. Of particular help were: Werner
Braun,Chris Falkenstein, Kevin Fosburg, Jim Howard, Bill Levanthal, Walt Shipley, Tucker
Tech and Jonny Woodward.

Contents

Dave Bengston on Reed's Direct

Walter J. Flint photo

Required Reading

YOSEMITE VALLEY CONTINUES TO REVEAL ITSELF as an incomparably beautiful and vast rock-sculptured wonder. Decade after decade, it has been an inspiring dream for climbers, and provided the fulfilling reality of a supreme granite-climbing experience. The number of climbers attracted to Yosemite, and the level of drama played out in this arena, is testimony to Yosemite's allure, as is the sheer number of routes established by these climbers. It is the aim of this book to distill from these numerous routes the essence of quality Yosemite climbing.

In such a renowned area as Yosemite, a significant number of routes stand out indisputably as classic in nature. Many others are included here because they have shown themselves to be popular, rewarding—and convenient to reach. Nonetheless, skimming a mere handful of routes out of the barrel clearly is a subjective process. Appraised with close to 20 years of climbing experience in Yosemite Valley, and by associating with the climbers of the valley, the author aims to provide a fun and rewarding sample of Yosemite climbing.

STAYING IN THE PARK

An entrance fee must be paid upon entering the park, which can be dealt with in one of three ways. Visitors can purchase a $20 one-week pass per car; a $40 Yosemite Pass, which allows yearly access to Yosemite only; or a $50 Golden Eagle Pass, which allows annual passage into national parks and monuments throughout the country. During the summer season, from June 1 to September 15, there is a seven-day camping limit in the valley. There is a 30-day limit the rest of the year.

The National Park Service is the governing authority within Yosemite, and the park service's obligation is the preservation of this national resource. Thus, the service is responsible for law enforcement, ambulance service, roads, campgrounds (although the reservation system is handled by Destinet), water, sewage, trash, etc. It also conducts search and rescue operations when necessary. Also, and not to be eclipsed by the above-mentioned, the park service also handles resource management and interpretive programs.

The concessionaire in Yosemite is the Yosemite Concession Services. It offers and operates virtually all of the goods and services within the park. The medical clinic, Ansel Adams Studio and an automatic teller machine are a few exceptions. A general store, post office, medical clinic, visitor center, garage and delicatessen are located in Yosemite Village. Curry Village, Yosemite Lodge and Ahwahnee Hotel provide accommodations ranging from modest tent-cabins to fairly luxurious hotel rooms. Additional public facilities can be found at these locations as well. At Yosemite Lodge, for instance, there is a year-round cafeteria, restaurant, bar and gift shop/convenience store. Of special interest, there are showers at Curry Village ($2.00, soap and towel provided). Also at Curry Village, there is a mountain shop, the Yosemite Mountaineering School and Guide Service, and the usual cafeteria, convenience store, fast food, etc. The laundromat can be found at Curry Housekeeping Camp. The only gas station currently in the valley is adjacent to Sunnyside Campground. However, there are plans to remove the gas station in the near future.

Four campgrounds are located in the valley. Sunnyside Campground (AKA Camp 4) is the place with the most atmosphere, and is the popular choice among climbers. In this boulder-strewn, walk-in campground, individuals are charged $3 per night for shared sites, with up to six people allowed in each site. It can be overflowing or deserted, depending on the time of year and weather conditions. Most of the other campgrounds provide conventional car camping, with sites going for $15 per night with a six-person, two-car maximum. Advance reservations for car camping are necessary from spring to mid-fall, particularly on weekends. Reservations may be made up to five months in advance, starting on the fifthteenth of each month. The mailing address for Destinet is 9450 Carroll Park Drive, San Diego, California 92121, or call Destinet toll-free at (800) 436-7275. From outside the U.S., call Destinet at 1(619) 452-8787. Mindful of the great demand for campsites in Yosemite Valley, callers are advised that the phone numbers become operational starting at 7:00 am Pacific Standard Time. Reservations also may be made in person at the campground Reservation Office in Curry Village. Pets are permitted in designated campgrounds (Upper Pines) only and must be leashed at all times. Pets are not allowed on any park trails.

A free shuttle bus system runs between the Lodge, Village, Ahwahnee and Curry, which provides easy access to climbs within the east end of the valley. Bicycles work well in the main valley, but for climbers without cars, arranging rides with other climbers may be necessary to get to cliffs in the lower valley.

Suggestions and Precautions

For the climber interested in bouldering, an excellent bouldering circuit extends from the western end of Camp 4 east to Swan Slab. Other prime bouldering spots are the start of the Four Mile Trail, below Sentinel Rock, and near the Curry Housekeeping Camp.

Poison oak is found throughout the valley, although it grows most abundantly west of the Pohono Bridge, and throughout the Lower Merced Canyon. Rattlesnakes may be encountered in warm weather months basking in the sun along the base of cliffs. Rarely do they provide more than a minor nuisance on an approach to a climb.

Environmental Issues:
The National Park Service Perspective

The National Park Service was created in 1916 to "provide for the enjoyment of the visitor" and to "leave the park unimpared for future generations." Unfortunately, these two goals often conflict, and balancing the immediate demands of visitors with the long-term health of the park is a task that often generates controversy. Climbers and non-climbers alike effect, and are affected by, Park Service land use policy.

Climbing is one of the oldest recreational uses in Yosemite, predating the establishment of the park in 1890. James Hutchings, John Muir, and Clarence King had little impact on the mountains they climbed, using no equipment that marred the rock and leaving nothing behind. With the exception of George Anderson's bolt route on the Northeast Face of Half Dome in 1875, this benign relationship prevailed until the 1930s, when the use of pitons, bolts, and other modern climbing methods became popular. Increasing numbers of climbers through the 1940s, 50s, and 60s led to noticable rock damage and the clean climbing revolution of the 70s.

Given the large number of climbers and the nature of the damage they cause, the Park Service has enacted surprisingly little regulation of the sport.This is partly due to the historic use of the park for climbing and partly because climbers have traditionally policed themselves. Indeed, for many years climbing and environmentalism were seen as close partners; until recently the "Sierra Club Bulletin" published climbing stories and route descriptions next to articles on preserving wilderness areas. Many of the outstanding conservationists in American history were climbers, notably Muir and David Brower. To Muir, the term "mountaineer" implied that one not only climbed and felt at home in the high country but loved and cared for the mountains as well.

This perception, however, has changed. Climbing is now seen by some people as just one more destructive use of the land. In several areas of the country, both private landowners and public land agencies have responded to climber-caused environmental damage by restricting climbing. The list of problems caused by climbers is lengthy: multiple approach trails and the subsequent erosion, disturbance of cliff dwelling animals, destruction of Native American rock art, litter, chalk marks, pin scars, bolts, chopped holds and aid placements, glued-on artificial holds, gardening (an ironic euphemism for destroying vegetation), "trails" of lichen-free rock that can be seen from miles away, bivy ledges that reek of urine and feces, chopping down trees close to a route, bright-colored rappel slings, etc. Virtually all of these impacts have occurred in Yosemite in the last few years. Some of these impacts are reversible (litter, feces, chalk) while some are permanent (bolts, chopped holds, pin scars).

No other users of the park are permitted to cause such damage. These practices not only degrade the natural environment and diminish the climbing experience but are also noticed by the non-climbing public. The average visitor to Yosemite expects to view the park's famous cliffs without seeing chalk marks, bolts, and rappel slings. Visitor complaints (from non-climbers and climbers) about this damage are common.

Look around you when you go climbing; is erosion turning that approach trail into a gully? Is there a maze of trails where one would do? Is your climbing route visible from across the valley as a white path up the lichen-covered rock? Note the absence of small trees, bushes and flowering plants that were there a few years ago. None of that will regrow overnight. (Soil formation and lichen growth can take hundreds of years.) Now extend the damage you've identified ahead a decade, a generation, or several generations. What will it look like then? (How many new routes will have gone up in that time?) Compare that future with what you think the park should look like. For how long do you think the park should be maintained in its natural state? Do your wishes match the changes you see around you?

Clearly, some limitations are necessary. Currently, motorized drilling, cutting trees, attaching artificial holds, and littering are illegal in the park. If present trends continue, more control of climbing activity may be required to protect the natural environment. If climbers undertake reforms themselves, additional regulations may not be necessary.

What can you do to protect the environment while preserving your climbing freedom? First, climb in an environmentally responsible manner. Minimize your impact. Follow the "Climber's Code" recently published by the Access Fund. Second, get involved. Write the park superintendent (NPS, PO Box 577, Yosemite, CA 95389) and express your opinions on climbing issues. Contact the Access Fund (303-545-6772) and local climbing groups. Third, exercise restraint. Just because a route can be climbed doesn't mean it should be climbed. Does El Cap really need another route with pitch after pitch of chiseled copperhead placements? Is it worth destroying hundreds of square feet of cliffside vegetation for yet another 5.11 face climb? Is it worth incurring public complaints by putting up another bolted route in Lower Falls Amphitheater? Is it really necessary to place bolts up a route that can be easily top-roped? Only by seriously considering such questions can Yosemite's walls and your freedom be preserved.

ETHICS AND CODE OF CONDUCT

Debates on climbing ethics rage on, and in Yosemite, ethics are argued with more fervor than just about anywhere else. There are a couple of reasons for this. First, the intrepid traditional character of climbing here is a philosophy deeply rooted in a long and treasured history. Second, being a national park, preservation of the resource is supposed to take priority over what is often seen as a special-interest pursuit with environmentally-damaging consequences. So, by skirting the enigma of climbing ethics, the focus here instead is to make a few points that hopefully will allow climbers to act more responsibly toward Yosemite.

• Don't scar, chisel, glue holds onto or otherwise deface natural rock.

• Don't place bolts next to cracks or other features that afford natural protection.

- Try to use colors that blend with the rock when leaving slings or equipment at rappel stations.
- Dispose of human waste properly.
- Don't throw haul bags or anything else off cliffs.
- Don't litter.
- Don't destroy natural vegetation.
- Use existing trails whenever possible.

Finally, it should be mentioned that keeping a low profile has proven the best method for enjoying an enduring, hassle-free stay in the valley.

STAYING ALIVE
JOHN DILL, NPS SEARCH AND RESCUE

Most climbers do a good job coping with the hazards of their sport, yet more than 100 climbing accidents occur in the park every year. What factors contribute to them? What, if anything, can climbers do to avoid them? And just how dangerous is climbing, anyway? With these questions in mind, the National Park Service (NPS) recently examined most of the serious accidents that occurred in the park during the 21 years from 1970 through 1990. The conclusions provide interesting reading for those wishing to stay alive.

Fifty-one climbers died from traumatic injuries in that period. A dozen more, critically hurt, would have died without rapid transport and medical treatment. In addition, there were many serious but survivable injuries, from fractured skulls to broken legs (at least 50 fractures per year), and a much larger number of cuts, bruises, and sprains.

Not surprisingly, most injuries occurred during leader falls and involved feet, ankles, or lower legs; for many, these are the accepted risks of climbing. However, leader falls accounted for only 25% of the fatal and near-fatal traumatic injuries; roughly 10% were from rockfall, 25% from being deliberately unroped, and 40% from simple mistakes with gear. Many cases are not clear cut; several factors may share the credit, and it is sometimes hard to quantify the weird adventures climbers have.

Not to be overlooked in the body count are environmental injuries. Inadequately equipped for the weather, four climbers died of hypothermia and perhaps 45 more would have died of the cold or the heat if not rescued.

Fifteen to 25 parties require an NPS rescue each year. Sixty more climbers stagger into Yosemite's medical clinic on their own, and an unknown number escape statistical immortality by seeking treatment outside the park (or at the Mountain Room Bar).

Most Yosemite victims are experienced climbers: 60% have been climbing for three years or more, lead at least 5.10, are in good physical condition, and climb frequently. Short climbs and big walls, easy routes and desperate ones—all get their share of the accidents.

The NPS keeps no statistics on how many climbers use the park, but 25,000 to 50,000 climber-days annually is a fair estimate. With this in mind, 2.5 deaths and a few serious injuries per year may seem a pretty low rate. It's much too high, however, if your climbing career is cut short by a broken hip, or worse. It's also too high when you consider that at least 80% of the fatalities, and many injuries, were easily preventable. In case after case, ignorance, a casual attitude, and/or some form of distraction proved to be the most dangerous aspects of the sport.

As the saying goes, "good judgement comes from bad experience." In the pages that follow are 21 years of condensed bad experience—the situations Yosemite climbers faced, the mistakes they made, and some recommendations for avoiding bad experiences of your own. This information comes in many cases from the victims' own analyses or from those of their peers.

Environmental Dangers

On Oct. 11, 1983, a climber on El Cap collapsed from heat exhaustion. On Oct. 11, 1984, a party on Washington Column was immobilized by hypothermia. You can expect this range of weather year-round.

Heat No Yosemite climber has died from the heat, but a half-dozen parties have come close. Too exhausted to move, they survived only because death by drying-up is a relatively slow process, allowing rescuers time to get there.

Temperatures on the sunny walls often exceed 100°F, but even in cool weather, climbing all day requires lots of water. The generally accepted minimum, two quarts per person per day, is just that—a minimum. It may not replace what you use, so don't let the desire for a light haulbag be your overriding concern, and take extra for unanticipated delays. Do not put all your water in a single container, and watch out for leaks.

If you find yourself rationing water, remember that dehydration will seriously sap your strength, slowing you even further. It's not uncommon to go from merely thirsty to a complete standstill in a single day. Continuing up may be the right choice but several climbers have said, "I should have gone down while I could."

Storms We still hear climbers say, "It never rains in Yosemite." In fact, there are serious storms year-round. Four climbers have died of hypothermia and almost 50 have been rescued, most of whom would not have survived otherwise. Several were very experienced, with winter alpine routes, Yosemite walls, and stormy bivouacs to their credit—experts, by most measures. In many cases they took sub-standard gear, added another mistake or two, and couldn't deal with the weather.

Mountain thunderstorms are common in spring, summer, and fall. They may appear suddenly out of a clear blue sky and rapidly shift position, their approach concealed by the route you are on. A few minutes warning may be all that you get. Thunderstorms may last only a couple of hours, but they are very intense, with huge amounts of near-freezing water often mixed with hail, strong winds, and lightning. The runoff can be a foot deep and fast enough to cause rockfall. A common result is a panicky retreat, a jammed rope, and cries for help. (The standard joke is that someone will drown on a Tuolumne climb one of these days. It's actually possible.)

No climber has died yet in such a storm because rescuers were able to respond. No climbers have died from lightning either, but there have been several near misses, and hikers on Half Dome and elsewhere have been killed. Get out of the way of a thunderstorm as fast as you can, and avoid summits and projections.

The big Pacific storm systems have proven more dangerous. They sweep through the Sierra at any time of year, most frequently from September through May. They are unpredictable, often appearing back-to-back after several weeks of gorgeous, mind-numbing weather. It may rain on Half Dome in January and snow there in July. These storms are dangerous because they are usually warm enough to be wet, even in winter, yet always cold enough to kill an unprotected climber. They last from one to several days, offering little respite if you can't escape.

With no soil to absorb it, rain on the walls quickly collects into streams and waterfalls, pouring off overhangs and down the corner you're trying to climb up or sleep in. Wind blows the water in all directions, including straight up. It may rip apart a plastic tube tent or blow a portaledge up and down until the tubing breaks or the fly rips. Overhanging faces and other "sheltered" spots are not always immune—rain and waterfalls several yards away may be blown directly onto your bivy, and runoff will wick down your anchor rope. Even a slow but steady leak into your shelter can defeat you. Temperatures may drop, freezing solid the next pitch, your ropes, and your wet sleeping bag.

Once cold and wet, you are in real trouble and your options run out. If you leave your shelter to climb or rappel, you deteriorate more rapidly from the wind and water. Even with good gear, water runs down your sleeve every time you reach up. As your body temperature drops, you begin making dumb mistakes, such as clipping in wrong or dropping your rack. You are seriously hypothermic, and soon you will just hang there, no longer caring. It happens quickly. In two separate incidents, climbers on the last pitch of the Nose left what protection they had to make a run for the top. They all died on that pitch.

Staying put may be no better. If you need help, no one may see you or hear you, and reaching you may take days longer than in good weather. Survivors say they had no idea how helpless they'd be until it happened to them. To find out for yourself, stand in the spray of a garden hose on a cold, windy night. How long will you last?

BIG WALL BIVOUACS   Despite this grim scenario, reasonable precautions will turn stormy big wall bivouacs into mere annoyances:

- Check the forecast just before you start up but don't rely on it. For several parties it provided no warning whatsoever.

- Assume you'll be hit by a storm, and that you'll not have a choice of bivvies.

- Ask friends to check on you if the weather or the forecast turns bad.

- Evaluate ahead of time the problems of retreat from any point on the route. Did you bring a bolt kit? How about a "cheater stick" for clipping into bolt hangers and stuffing cams into out-of-reach cracks as you flee down an overhanging pitch?

- If it's starting to rain, think twice about climbing "just one more pitch"—once wet you won't dry out. It's better to set up your bivy while you're still dry.

- Frozen ropes are useless for climbing or retreating, as several parties found out. Put them away early.

All such hints and tricks aside, the bottom line is your ability to sit out the storm. Your first priority is to keep the wind and outside water away. Second is to be insulated enough to stay warm, even though you are wet from your own condensation.

- Stick with high quality gear in good condition, and don't leave key items behind to ease the hauling. Don't go up with a poorly equipped partner; it will be your neck as well.

- For insulation, never rely on cotton or down (even if covered with one of the waterproof/breathable fabrics). Even nylon absorbs water. Wool, polypropylene, and polyester insulators stay relatively warm when wet, and the synthetics dry fastest. Take long underwear, warm pants, sweater, jacket, balaclava/hat, gloves, sleeping bag, insulating pad, extra socks or booties, and plenty of food and water—dehydration hastens hypothermia.

- For the rain, use coated nylon, sailors' oilskins, or the waterproof/breathable fabrics. Take rain pants and jacket, overmitts, bivy bag, and hammock or portaledge with waterproof fly. The fly is critical—it must overlap your hammock generously and be made of heavy material, in excellent condition, with strong, well-sealed seams. For sleeping on ledges, take a big tent fly or a piece of heavy-duty, reinforced plastic and the means to pitch it. Then hope that your ledge doesn't turn into a lake. Do you know how to run your anchor through the fly without making a hole? Did you spend more for lycra than rainwear?

- **Warning**: Several climbers have blamed the waterproof/breathable fabrics for their close calls. They claim that no version of it can take the punishment of a storm on the walls. Whether true or not, you must be the judge; test all of your gear ahead of time under miserable conditions, but where your exit is an easy one.

For more information on bad weather, including a description of the waterproof anchor, see "Surviving Big Walls," by Brian Bennett, *Climbing,* Feb./Mar. 1990.

UNPLANNED BIVOUACS   Getting caught by darkness is common, especially on the longer one-day climbs and descent routes, e.g., Royal Arches and Cathedral Rocks. It happens easily—a late start, a slow partner, off route, a jammed or dropped rope, or a sprained ankle. Usually it's nothing to get upset about, but if you are unprepared, even a cold wind or a mild storm becomes serious. One death and several close calls occurred this way. To avoid becoming a statistic:

- Consider the following gear for each person's day pack: long underwear, gloves, balaclava, rain jacket and pants (which double as wind protection). In warmer weather, equipment can be the lightweight variety. If that's too heavy for you, at least take one of those disposable plastic rainsuits or tube tents that occupy virtually no space. Take more warm clothes in colder weather. A headlamp with spare bulb and new batteries is very important for finding safe anchors, signaling for help, or avoiding that bivy altogether. Matches and heat-tabs will light wet wood. Food and water increase your safety after a night of shivering.

- Keep your survival gear with you whenever practical, not with your partner. Climbers get separated from their gear, and each other in imaginative ways, sometimes with serious consequences.

- Standing in slings on poor anchors is not the way to spend a night. If a bivy is inevitable, don't climb until the last moment; find a safe, sheltered, and/or comfortable spot while you've got enough light.

DESCENTS   Consult the guidebook and your friends, but be wary of advice that the way down is obvious; look the route over ahead of time. If you carry a topo of the way up, consider one for the way down, or a photograph. Your ultimate protection is route-finding ability, and that takes experience. Some trouble spots: North Dome Gully, the Kat Walk, Michael's Ledge.

- Many rappel epics are born when an easy descent, often a walk- off, is missed. Search for it thoroughly before you commit to a big drop—it may be well worth the effort.

- Conversely, footprints and rappel anchors often lead nowhere—they were someone else's mistake. Be willing and able to retrace your steps and remember that the crux may not be at the top.

- To further evaluate an uncertain descent, consider rappelling a single line as far as possible (160 feet if one rope, 320 feet if two). Learn to be comfortable on the rope and be willing to swing around a corner to look for the next anchor. Carry enough gear to go back up your rope and know how to use it.

- Any time you can't see anchors all the way to the ground, take the gear to set your own. That includes established descents, since ice and rockfall frequently destroy anchors. It sometimes means carrying a bolt kit.

- Consider taking a second (7-9mm) rope, even for one-rope descents and walk-offs. You'll save time, depend on fewer anchors, leave less gear, and more easily reverse the climbing route in an emergency. This is one advantage of leading on double ropes. But don't forget that thinner ropes are more vulnerable to sharp edges.

- Friction from wet or twisted ropes, slings, ledges, cracks and flakes may jam your rope. Plan ahead when you rig the anchor and be willing to leave gear behind to avoid friction. You can retrieve the gear tomorrow.

- Rappelling through trees? Consider short rappels, from tree to tree. It's slow but avoids irretrievable snarls.

- Is your rope jammed? You can go back up and rerig if you still have both ends, so keep them until you're sure it will pull or you have to let go. If you do have to climb that rope, be careful that it isn't jammed by a sharp edge. Don't forget to untie the knots in the ends before you pull.

- Dropped ropes and gear can be more than just embarrassing; without a rescue, a stranded climber is a dead climber, even in good weather. When transferring gear, clip it to its next anchor before unclipping it from the current one.

LOOSE ROCK   There's plenty of it in Yosemite. Ten percent of all injuries are associated with rockfall, including six deaths and one permanent disability. In several other deaths, loose rock was implicated but not confirmed, e.g., possible broken handholds and failed placements. Spontaneous rockfall is not the problem—all the fatal and serious accidents were triggered by the victim, the rope, or by climbers above.

Rocks lying on ledges and in steep gullies are obviously dangerous. Not so obvious is that old, reliable mantle block, five times your weight, wedged in place, and worn smooth by previous climbers. Yet with distressing regularity, "bombproof" blocks, flakes, and even ledges collapse under body weight, spit out cams, or fracture from the pressure of a piton. The forces placed on anchors and protection even from rappelling may be far higher than you generate in a test. Handholds may pass your scrutiny, then fail in mid-move. The rock you pull off can break your leg after falling only a couple of feet. Finally, watch out for rotten rock, responsible for at least two of these fatalities. It's common on the last couple of pitches of climbs that go to the rim of the valley, e.g., Yosemite Point Buttress and Washington Column.

The East Buttress of Middle Cathedral Rock is a well-known bowling alley and the site of many rockfall injuries. The Northwest Face of Half Dome is another, with the added excitement of tourist "firing squads" on the summit. But the most dangerous, surprisingly, may be El Cap; on rock so steep, loose blocks balance precariously and big flakes wait for an unlucky hand to trigger the final fracture.

Some rockfall accidents may not be preventable, short of staying home, but being alert to the hazard and following a few guidelines will cut the injury rate:

- Consider a helmet for loose routes. (See Helmets, p.14.)

- Throw in an occasional piece on long, easy runouts, as insurance against the unpredictability of the medium.

- Avoid rotten rock as protection, even if you can back it up. When it fails it endangers everyone below.

- Ropes launch almost as many missiles as climbers do. Watch where you run your lead rope. Use directionals to keep it away from loose—and sharp—stuff, and check it frequently. Keep in mind that your bag or pack, when hauled, may dislodge everything in its path. When you pull your rappel ropes, stand to one side, look up, and watch out for delayed rockfall.

- You have no control over a party above you, and by being below you accept the risk. If you are catching up, don't crowd them—ask for permission to pass. You can probably get by them safely, but remember that climbers have been killed or hurt by rocks dislodged by parties above, including those they allowed to pass. The party you want to pass may have gotten an early start to avoid that risk, and they have no obligation to let you by. When you are above someone else, including your partner, put yourself in their shoes. Slow down, watch your feet and the rope.

Cloud's Rest and Half Dome

Walter J. Flint photo

CLIMBING UNROPED

Everybody does it, to some extent. There's no reason to stop, but good reason to be cautious: fourteen climbers were killed and two critically injured while deliberately unroped. At least eight climbed 5.10 or better. Most, if not all, of those accidents were avoidable. You may find yourself unroped in several situations: on third-class terrain, spontaneously on fifth-class, and while deliberately free-soloing a route.

Third-class terrain may be easy, but add a bit of sand, loose or wet rock, darkness, plus a moment of distraction, and the rating becomes meaningless. Four climbers have died this way, typically on approach and descent routes such as North Dome Gully, all in spots that did not demand a rope.

Sometimes you lose the way on the approach, or unrope at what you thought was the top of the climb, only to find a few feet of "easy" fifth-class blocking your way. Your rope is tucked away in your pack, and you're in a hurry. Before you go on, remember that you didn't plan to free-solo an unknown quantity today. Four died this way, falling from fifth-class terrain that they were climbing on the spur of the moment.

Seven of the 14 killed were rappelling or otherwise tied in. They unroped while still on fifth-class rock, for various reasons of convenience, without clipping into a nearby anchor. Three slipped off their stances, a ledge collapsed under another, one decided to down-climb the last few feet, and two tried to climb their rappel ropes hand-over-hand to attend to some problem. Like the previous group, they all went unroped onto fifth-class terrain on the spur of the moment. In addition, they all had a belay immediately available. Did its nearness give them a false sense of security?

No true free-soloer has been killed yet, although one, critically hurt, survived only by the speed of his rescue. A death will happen eventually, possibly the result of a loose hold. Is the free-soloer more alert to the task having planned it in advance, than those who unroped on the spur of the moment? Were the unlucky still relaxed in their minds, not quite attuned to their new situation? We can only speculate.

Keep these cases and the hidden hazards in mind as you travel through any steep terrain. Be aware of what is under foot, and in hand, at each moment. Be patient enough to retrace your steps to find the easy way, and if there's a belay hanging in front of you, think twice before rejecting it. Finally, remember that your climbing ability has probably been measured on clean, rated routes, not on unpredictable sand and wet moss. Being a 5.11 climber does not mean you can fly.

LEADING

Nine climbers died and six were critically injured in leader-fall accidents involving inadequate protection. Most fell simply because the moves were hard, and several were victims of broken holds. They were all injured because they hit something before their protection stopped them. Either they did not place enough protection (one-third of the cases) or it failed under the force of the fall (the remaining two-thirds). In every case, their injuries were serious because they fell headfirst or on their sides—the head, neck, or trunk took a lethal blow. Half fell 50 feet or less, the climber falling the shortest distance (25 feet) dying, and the longest (270 feet!) surviving.

Were these catastrophes avoidable? It's sometimes hard to tell, but the answer is often yes. Here are a few lessons frequently learned the hard way:

- Climbers frequently describe the belaying habits they see on Yosemite routes as "frightening." Before you start up, how frightening is your belay? Can the anchor withstand pulls in all directions? Is there more than one piece, with the load shared? Is the tie-in snug and in line with the fall force? Is your belayer experienced with that belay gadget and in position to operate it effectively when you fall? (You'd be surprised.) Will you clip through a bombproof directional as you start up, even on an easy pitch?

- Don't cheat on your ground fall calculations. (A good belayer will keep you honest.) With rope stretch and slack in the system, you may fall twice as far below your last protection as you are above it—if it holds.

- Nuts want to fall out. One that self-cleans below you may turn a comfortable lead into a ground-fall situation. Or, during a fall, the top piece may hold just long enough for the rope to yank the lower nuts out sideways, and then also fail. For more reliable placements, set those nuts with a tug and sling them generously. A tug on a marginal nut, however, is worthless as a test. Tiny nubbins may hold it firmly under those conditions but give way in a fall. Be especially cautious about placements you can't see. Back them up.

- Camming devices "fail" regularly, but it's seldom the fault of the device. It's more likely due to haste, coupled with undeserved faith in technology. As with nuts, a blind placement—often in a layback crack—may feel solid but be worthless.

- Fixed pitons loosen from freeze-thaw cycles and repeated use. They may not have been installed well to begin with. A hammer is the only reliable way to test and reset them, but you don't see many hammers on free routes these days. You don't see them on rappel routes either, but you may find yourself hanging from anchors that belong in a museum. If you don't test pitons properly, do not depend on them—routinely back them up.

- There is no reliable way to test bolts but plenty of reasons to want to. For example, the common ¼" split-shaft type was not designed or intended for life support, let alone for rock climbing. Their quality varies; several have broken under body weight, and others like them await you. Reliability also depends on the quality of the rock and the skill of the bolter. Add years of weathering and mistreatment by climbers and the result is many bolts that are easily pulled out by fingers or a sharp yank with a sling. Several bolt hangers have cracked as well, with one fatal accident so far.

- Never test a bolt with a hammer. Instead, examine the surrounding rock, the bolt, and the hanger for cracks, and hope they are large enough to see. Is the bolt tight and fully seated in the hole? Is the nut snug? Good luck.

- Back up all untested, fixed protection.

- Okay. So you know this stuff. You're a little shaky on the lead right now and you've had some trouble getting your pro to stick, but the book said this was 5.10a, and besides, two teenage girls just walked up this pitch. It's only 20 feet more and one of those pieces is bound to hold. Think for a minute. Are you willing to free-solo this pitch? Keep your answer in mind as you climb, because poorly placed protection amounts to just that—you may not be deliberately unroped, but you might as well be.

ABOUT FALLING   There's an art to falling safely—like a cat. Bouldering helps build the alertness required. Controlling your fall may be out of the question on those 200-foot screamers, but it will reduce the risk of injury from routine falls. Whenever possible, land on your feet—even if you break your leg. Absorbing the shock this way may save your life. Laybacks and underclings hold special risks in this regard. You are already leaning back, and if you lose your grip the friction of your feet on the rock may rotate you into a headfirst—and backward—dive.

- A chest harness will not keep you from tumbling as you free-fall, but it will turn you upright as the rope comes tight. This reduces the chance of serious injury during the braking phase and may be life-saving if you hang there for long, already seriously hurt.

- The wall may look vertical below you, but even glancing off a steep slab can be fatal. Three climbers died this way.

- Pendulum falls are particularly dangerous. If you swing into a corner from 20 feet to one side of your protection, you will hit with the same bone-breaking speed as when striking a ledge in a 20 foot vertical fall. The crucial difference is, you are "landing" on your side, exposing vital organs to the impact. Two climbers died this way and others suffered serious injuries. Even small projections are dangerous; a 20 foot swing on Glacier Pt. Apron fractured a skull, and another smashed a pelvis. In a pendulum there is no difference between a leader and a follower fall; don't forget to protect your second from this fate as you lead a hard traverse.

LEARNING TO LEAD   Four of the 15 killed or critically injured in leader falls were good climbers on well-defined routes, but the majority were intermediates, often off route. There may be a couple of lessons in that.

- Don't get cocky because you just led your first 5.8 or your protection held on your first fall. Experienced climbers have died from errors "only a beginner would make," so you have plenty of time left in your career to screw up.

- Climbing and protecting are separate skills but both keep you alive. Don't challenge yourself in both at the same time—you may not have the skill and presence of mind to get out of a tight spot. If you're out to push your limits, pick a route that's well defined and easy to protect, place extra pieces for practice, and be willing and equipped to back off.

- Routefinding is another survival skill. A mistake here can quickly put you over your head in climbing, protecting, or both. Learn to look ahead and recognize what you want to avoid. Climb it mentally before you climb it physically.

- Some "easy" terrain in the valley is actually pretty dangerous. Low-angle gullies are often full of loose blocks cemented together with moss. Opportunities for protection may be scarce and routefinding subtle. These are not usually cataloged routes. Three or four climbers have been killed, or nearly so, on such terrain while looking for easy routes to climb.

- **A Leading Problem:** The last pitch of the Nutcracker provides a subtle challenge for the fledging 5.8 leader. Once over the mantle, you may relax as you contemplate the easy climb to the top. But if you forget about your protection, a slip in the next few moves may send you back over the side to crash into the slab below. This pitch has scored several broken ankles when the fall was longer than expected, and a more serious injury is possible. There are many such situations in the valley, and one key to safety is to look below you while you plan ahead.

THE BELAY CHAIN

Whether you are climbing, rappelling, or just sitting on a ledge, the belay chain is what connects you to the rock. There are many links, and mistakes with almost every one have killed 22 climbers, 40% of all Yosemite climbing fatalities. In every case the cause was human error. In every case the death was completely preventable, not by the subtle skills of placing protection on the lead, but by some simple precaution to keep the belay chain intact. Experienced climbers outnumbered the inexperienced in this category, two to one.

Mistakes with the belay chain can occur at any time. Make one and you'll fall to the end of the rope ... or farther. Minor injuries are rare. Here are some key points to remember:

- Before you commit yourself to a system, always apply a few pounds of tension in the directions in which it will be loaded, analyzing it like an engineer—what if this happens ... or that? Check every link, from the buckle of your harness to the rock around your anchor. You would be amazed at the inadequate systems often used by experienced climbers, even though it takes only a few seconds to run a proper check.

- Both lives depend on that system, so go through it with your partner. Nine climbers have died in multi-victim accidents.

- Check the system periodically while you're using it. Forces may change direction (two died when their anchors failed for this reason), ropes and slings can wear through (serious injuries and one death) and gear can come undone (two died when a wiggling bolt hanger unscrewed its nut—they were relying on a single bolt.)

- Are you about to rappel? Stay clipped to the anchor for a few seconds. Check the anchor and your brake system, as indicated. If one anchor point fails, will you remain attached to others? Are the knots in your rappel slings secure? Did you check every inch of those fixed slings for damage? Skipping these precautions cost eight deaths plus serious injuries from: poorly tied slings; partially dismantled anchors (a simple misunderstanding); relying on single carabiners; and other reasons. The next accident may be caused by something new, but it will have been preventable by double-checking.

- Two climbers died by rappelling off the ends of their ropes, even though both had tied knots in the ends as a safety measure. In one case the knots pulled through the brake. In the second, the victim forgot to double-check the ropes after a knot had been untied to deal with a problem. Knots are still a recommended safety procedure, but do not take anything for granted. Tie both strands into one knot or knot each separately. There are pros and cons to each method.

- When rappelling in unpredictable circumstances—dark, windy, poor communications, unknown anchors below—consider a Prusik Hitch or a mechanical ascender as a safety. If improperly handled, neither one may stop you if you fall—they are primarily used for quickly but deliberately stopping yourself to deal with other emergencies. Both of those who rappelled off their ropes would have survived with safeties.

- In separate incidents, five climbers somehow became detached from their ropes while climbing with mechanical ascenders—not the fault of the devices. Only three were tied to their ropes at all, at the lower end. All five died because they had not tied in "short," leaving themselves open to a long fall. To tie in short, tie a loop in the rope a few feet below your ascenders and clip it to your harness. As you climb, repeat the process often enough to limit your fall should you come off your rope. At the very least, do this when you must pass one ascender around protection, traverse (three deaths), or change to another rope. (Is that other rope anchored well? One climber died partly because his wasn't. Ask your partner first.) In addition, always be tied into both of your ascenders.

- Self-belayers should also tie in short. One died when his Prusik belay melted during a fall (a Prusik cord too large for the rope). At least two were treated to close calls when other types of self-belay systems jammed open.

- Clip into a new belay point before unclipping from the old one. During those few, vulnerable seconds, pitons have pulled, hero loops have broken, rocks have struck, and feet have slipped.

- Three climbers were killed and one critically injured by "failures" of single-carabiner tie-ins and rappel anchors. Be careful of relying on a single non-locking carabiner for any link in the chain. The rope or sling may flip over the gate and unclip itself, especially if it is slack, or shock-loaded. Even if you watch it carefully and/or it is "safely" under tension, you may become distracted. One died when his Figure Eight descender unclipped while he was busy passing a knot on rappel. (He should have tied in short.) For those critical points, use either two non-locking carabiners with gates opposed and reversed, or a locking carabiner. Don't forget to lock it! For many applications the two-carabiner method is safer, and faster to operate.

- Ropes have been cut in three fatal accidents. They did not break, but were stressed over sharp edges, a condition never intended by the manufacturer. Two of these accidents were avoidable: one climber should have tied in short to prevent a 100 foot fall that cut the rope; the other should have protected a fixed rope from a well-defined sharp edge. Ascending a rope produces a weighted, see-sawing action that can destroy it, even over a rounded, moderately rough, edge.

- As with ropes, most gear failure falls into the misuse category. Failure from a design or manufacturing flaw is rare. It was the initiating factor in one fatal accident, and three climbers died when a bolt hanger broke at a two-bolt rappel anchor. The tragic outcome would have been avoided, however, had the climbers noticed they were not properly backed up to the second bolt.

These cases illustrate one of the rules most commonly overlooked: BACK YOURSELF UP. No matter what initially pulled, broke, slipped, jammed, or cut, the incident became an accident because the climber did not carefully ask himself, "What if . . . ?" By leaving yourself open, you are betting against a variety of unpredictable events. You don't lose very often, but when you do, you may lose very big.

BEGINNERS!   From your first day on the rock, you have the right to inspect, and ask questions about, any system to which you're committing your life. It's a good way to learn, and a good way to stay alive. If your partner or instructor is offended, find someone else to climb with. Never change the system or the plan, however, without your partner's knowledge.

HELMETS

While we can never know for certain, helmets might have made a difference in roughly 25% of the fatal and critical trauma cases. They would have significantly increased—but not guaranteed—the survival chances for five of those fatalities. Furthermore, helmets would have offered excellent protection against less serious fractures, concussions, and lacerations.

Most deaths, however, involved impacts of overwhelming force or mortal wounds other than to the head, i.e., beyond the protection offered by a helmet. This is not an argument against helmets; the point is, a helmet doesn't make you invincible. What goes on inside your head is more important than what you wear on it.

When to wear a helmet is a personal choice, but it is especially recommended for the following: beginners pushing their skills, roped solo climbing, a high risk of a bad fall or of ice fall (several El Cap routes in winter and spring), and for all approaches, descents, and climbing routes that are crowded and/or particularly loose. (See Loose Rock, p. 8.)

STATES OF MIND

This is the key to safety. It's impossible to know how many climbers were killed by haste or overconfidence, but many survivors will tell you that they somehow lost their good judgement long enough to get hurt. It's a complex subject and sometimes a touchy one. Nevertheless, at least three states of mind frequently contribute to accidents: ignorance, casualness, and distraction.

IGNORANCE   There is always more to learn, and even the most conscientious climber can get into trouble if unaware of the danger ("I thought it never rained . . . "). Here are some ways to fight ignorance:

- Look in the mirror. Are you the stubborn type? Do you resist suggestions? Could you be a bit overconfident? (Ask your friends.) Several partners have said of a dead friend, "I wanted to give him advice, but he always got mad when I did that. I didn't realize he was about to die."

- Read. The climbing magazines are full of good recommendations. Case histories in the American Alpine Club's *Accidents in North American Mountaineering,* a yearly compilation of accident reports, will show you how subtle factors may combine to catch you unaware. Such accounts are the next best (or worst?) thing to being there.

- Practice. Reading may make you aware but not competent. In fact, you can be dangerously misled by what you read, including this report. Important details are often left out, the advice may be incorrect, and in the long run you must think and act for yourself. Several climbers, for example, waited to learn Prusiking until it was dark, raining, overhanging and already in trouble. They had read about it, but they had to be rescued despite having the gear to improvise their own solutions. Book-learning alone gave them a complacency that could have proved fatal.

CASUALNESS "I just didn't take it seriously," is a common lament. It's often correct, but it's more a symptom than a cause—there may be deeper reasons for underestimating your risk. Ignorance is one, and here are some more:

- Habit reinforcement. The more often you get away with risky business the more entrenched your lazy habits become. Have you unconsciously dropped items from your safety checklists since you were a chicken-hearted (or hare-brained) beginner?

- Your attitudes and habits can be reinforced by the experiences (and states of mind) of others. The sense of awe and commitment of the 1960s is gone from the big wall trade routes, and young aspirants with no Grade VI's, or even V's, to their credit speak casually about them. Even for experts, most accidents on El Cap occur on the easier pitches, where their guard is down.

- Memory Decay. "I'm not going up again without raingear—I thought I would die!" A week later this climber had forgotten how scared he had been in that thunderstorm. Raingear was now too heavy and besides, he was sure he'd be able to rap off the next time. Many of us tend to forget the bad parts. We have to be hit again.

- Civilization. With fixed anchors marking the way up and ghetto blasters echoing behind, it may be hard to realize that the potential for trouble is as high in Yosemite as anywhere. Some say the possibility of fast rescue added to their casualness. Maybe, but who wants a broken leg, or worse, in the first place?

DISTRACTION It is caused by whatever takes your mind off your work—anxiety, sore feet, skinny-dippers below—the list is endless. Being in a hurry is one of the most common causes. Here are two ways it has happened:

- Experienced climbers were often hurt after making "beginner errors" (their words) to get somewhere quickly. There was no emergency or panic, but their minds were elsewhere: on a cold beer, a good bivy, or just sick of being on that route for a week. (It's often called "summit fever.") Their mistakes were usually short cuts in protecting easy pitches, on both walls and shorter climbs. As one put it, "We were climbing as though we were on top."

- Darkness had caught two day-climbers for the first time. Unprepared, upset, and off route, they rushed to get down, arguing with each other about what to do. After several errors, which they knew how to avoid, one died rappelling off the end of his rope.

An adequate state of mind is like good physical conditioning; it doesn't happen overnight, and it takes constant practice, but the payoff in both safety and fun is well worth it. Stay aware of your mental state: Are you uneasy before this climb? Learn to recognize that, then ask yourself why, and deal with it. Are you taking shortcuts on this pitch? Could it be you're distracted? Stop, get your act together, then go.

RESCUE

- Despite the best of attitudes, an accident can happen to anyone. Self-rescue is often the fastest and safest way out, but whether it's the wise course of action depends on the injury and how well prepared you are. Combining with a nearby party will often give you the margin of safety you need, but do not risk aggravating an injury or getting yourselves into a more serious predicament—ask for help if you need it. (Sometimes a bit of advice, delivered by loudspeaker, is all that's required.) In making your decision, keep an eye on weather and darkness—call for help early.

- If you don't have formal first aid training (which is strongly recommended), at least know how to keep an unconscious patient's airway open, how to protect a possible broken neck or back, and how to deal with external bleeding and serious blood loss. These procedures are lifesaving, do not require fancy gear, and are easy to learn.

- Head injury victims, even when unconscious, may try to untie themselves. If you have to leave one alone, make escape impossible.

- If ropes are lowered to you from a helicopter for any purpose, do not attach them to your anchors unless you are specifically instructed to do so—if the helicopter has to leave suddenly it could pull you off the wall. If you are told to anchor a rope, rescuers will be using a system that does not expose you to that risk; anchor that rope securely—it may be a rescuer's lifeline. Follow instructions exactly.

WHO PAYS FOR RESCUES? The taxpayer does; the NPS does not charge for the cost of rescues, except for any ambulance services required. This is true even if you are fined by the courts for negligence, which is a separate charge altogether (see below). But rescues can be expensive and what the future holds is anybody's guess. The NPS is examining the possibility of charging all victims for the full cost of their rescues, and partial costs are charged in some parks now. This issue is complex, but it is clear that responsible behavior by those who use the park will minimize the threat.

RISK, RESPONSIBILITY, AND THE LIMITS TO CLIMBING

The NPS has no regulations specifying how you must climb. There is one regulation, however, requiring that all park users act responsibly. This applies to climbers, in that the consequences of your actions put rescuers and other climbers at risk. One rescuer has been killed in the park, so far. Thus, if your own negligence got you into trouble, you may be charged with "creating a hazardous condition" for others. As an example, a climber was fined because he became stranded by a hailstorm while attempting to free-solo the Steck-Salathe on Sentinel Rock. Storms had been predicted, and his rescue should not have been necessary.

Even avoidable accidents are understandable, thus legal charges are not frequently filed. Of all park users, however, climbers should be particularly aware. They know that their sport is dangerous, that safety lies in education and training, and that there is an information network available.

So take what you'll need with you on the climb, or have competent friends ready to back you up. The climber stranded on Sentinel, for example, could have been rescued by friends without NPS participation or knowledge—the way it must often be done on expeditions. Freedom of expression and responsibility need not be incompatible.

Climbing will always be risky. It should be clear, however, that a reduced accident rate is possible without seriously restricting the sport. The party in its fifth day on the Nose and the party passing them in its fifth hour may each be climbing safely or be blindly out of control. You have a right to choose your own climbing style and level of risk, but you owe it to yourself and everyone else to make that choice with your eyes wide open.

OTHER NOTES

VOLUNTARY REGISTRATION SYSTEM If you wish, you may register at the Valley Visitor Center before your climb. However, the NPS does not monitor your progress at any time; the registration information you provide is used only if someone reports that you are overdue. Your best insurance is a friend who checks on you frequently.

TO REPORT AN EMERGENCY From a public phone, dial 911. No money is needed to make the call. Stay at the phone until a ranger arrives, unless you are specifically given other instructions.

ACCIDENT/HAZARD REPORTING If you know of dangerous route conditions such as loose rock or bad anchors, consider posting the information on the bulletin board at Camp 4 (irreverently called Sunnyside by the NPS). Your information will help other climbers.

FIXED GEAR WARNING The park is a Wilderness Area, not an urban climbing wall. The NPS does not inspect or maintain climbing or descent routes, including fixed anchors, loose rock or any other feature. You are strictly on your own.

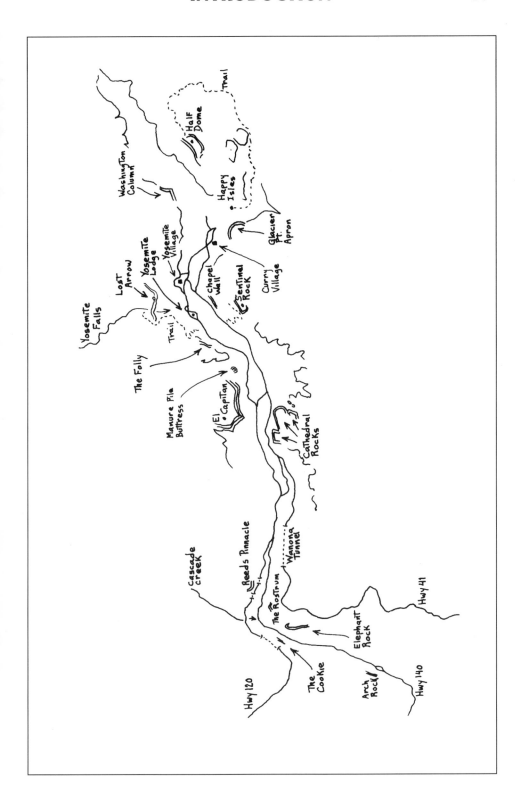

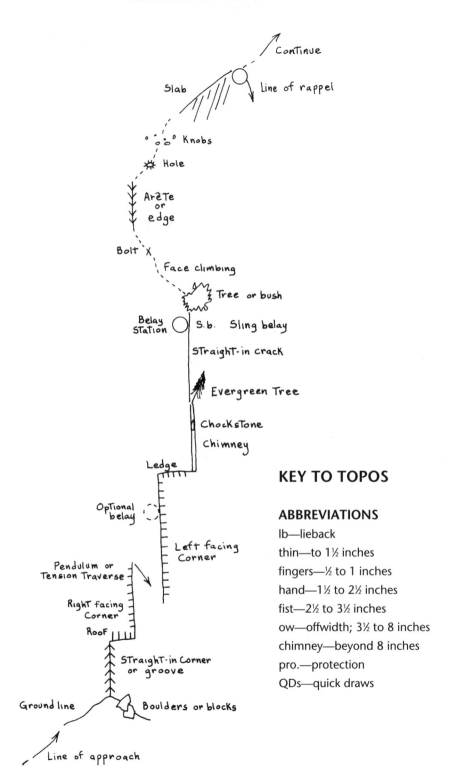

Continue

Line of rappel

Slab

Knobs

Hole

Arête or edge

Bolt

Face climbing

Tree or bush

Belay Station

S.b.   Sling belay

Straight-in crack

Evergreen Tree

Chockstone

Chimney

Ledge

Optional belay

Left facing Corner

Pendulum or Tension Traverse

Right facing Corner

Roof

Straight-in Corner or groove

Ground line

Boulders or blocks

Line of approach

KEY TO TOPOS

ABBREVIATIONS

lb—lieback
thin—to 1½ inches
fingers—½ to 1 inches
hand—1½ to 2½ inches
fist—2½ to 3½ inches
ow—offwidth; 3½ to 8 inches
chimney—beyond 8 inches
pro.—protection
QDs—quick draws

TOSSING HAULBAGS   Do not throw your haul bag off a wall. You cannot always be sure the coast is clear, and the bag will drift in the wind. No one has been hurt yet, but it will happen—there have been a few close calls. Bag-tossing also creates a carnival atmosphere, a big mess (of your gear), and lots of false alarms for rescuers. (Tourists usually think it's a body.)

SOURCES OF INFORMATION   Try the local climbers, found in the parking lot at Camp 4, the bulletin board at the Camp 4 kiosk, the Mountain Shop, the Visitor Center at Yosemite Village, any ranger, or the NPS library (next to the Visitor Center). The library is the home of the American Alpine Club's Sierra Nevada Branch Library. It carries magazines, journals, and books on all aspects of climbing, mountaineering, and natural history.

HOW TO USE THIS BOOK

The routes in this book are arranged in geographical order, starting from the west end of the north side of the valley, then moving to the south side, from east to west. (Refer to map on p. 17.)

Confusion could arise from the existence of other routes not presented in this selected guide. Often, bolts on adjacent, unlisted routes are shown simply as landmarks of the area.

The term arête is stretched far beyond its true definition in this book to mean any edge formed by two planes of rock, regardless of the mechanics of creation.

Although all routes in this guide are considered to be of good quality, some extend to excellence. A star quality rating is used to better identify various appealing aspects of a climb. In the past, certain routes, even without a star rating, have seen climbing parties stacked up in line, vying for position. Safety, common sense and courtesy must prevail in encounters with other climbers on the same or intersecting routes. The potential for accidents, personal and logistical friction, as well as long-term repercussions of park service involvement in climber problem areas warrants that climbers act responsibly.

ARCH ROCK

From the parking area at the entrance station, walk up the road to a clearing adjacent to the power lines. Class-two talus leads directly up to the base of Midterm.

A   **Anticipation   5.11b**   ★★   Pro to 3½ inch, including two each ⅛ inch to ¾ inch—3 to 3½ inch useful at first belay. Stemming, crack switch, reaching through for finger locks at the crux.

B   **T.K.O.   5.11c**   ★★   Pro: QDs and a few pieces, including a #3½ Friend.

C   **Punchline   5.12c** ★★   Pro: QDs and a few pieces plus a #3½ Friend.

Both routes step out of the fist crack above the tree onto the sublimely-featured arête.

Heated controversy surrounding these rap routes has resulted in smashed bolt hangers that have since been re-straightened. This is the case on T.K.O., at least.

D   **Midterm   5.10b** ★★★   Pro: ⅛ to 3½ inch. An ever-widening polished crack.

E   **Leanie Meanie 5.11b** ★★★ Pro: ¾ to 3½ inch, especially 1 to 2½ inch. A #11 Hex is useful. Ever-widening, leaning crack. Steep and clean.

F   **Gripper   5.10b** ★★★   Pro: ⅛ to 3½ inch. Varied crack climbing with an emphasis on hand-jamming. The third pitch is amazing.

G   **New Dimensions 5.11a** ★★★   Pro: ⅛ to 3 inch. The second and third pitches each have a section of awkward, physical climbing. A superb crack system with a climactic final move.

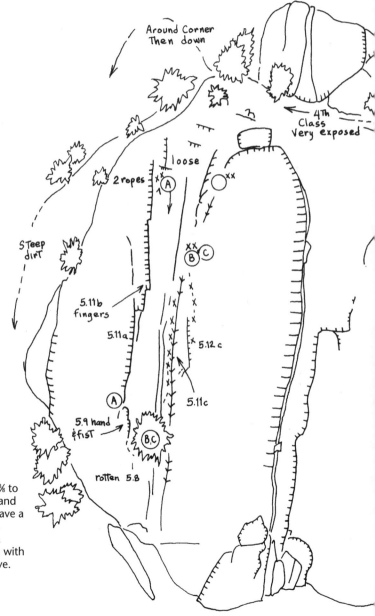

Around Corner
Then down

4Th Class
Very exposed

loose

2 ropes   A

B C

5.11b fingers

5.11a

5.12 c

STeep dirt

A

5.11c

5.9 hand & fisT

B,C

rotten 5.8

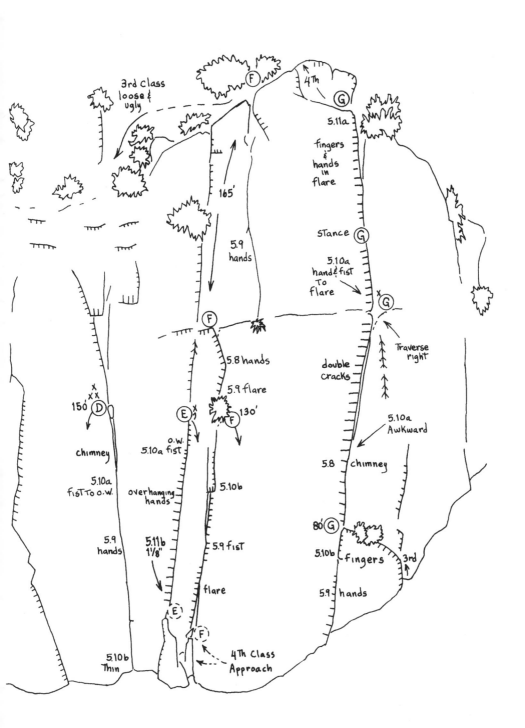

3rd class
loose &
ugly

F

4th

G

5.11a

fingers
&
hands
in
flare

165'

5.9
hands

stance G

5.10a
hand & fist
To
flare

F

Traverse
right

5.8 hands

double
cracks

5.9 flare

150' D
X
X X

E X
F 130'

5.10a
Awkward

chimney

O.W.
5.10a fist

5.8 chimney

5.10a
fist To o.w.

overhanging
hands

5.10b

80' G

5.9
hands

5.11b
1⅛"

5.9 fist

5.10b fingers

3rd

flare

5.9 hands

E

F

5.10b
Thin

4th Class
Approach

FINGER LICKIN' CLIFF

From a turnout 1 mile east of the Arch Rock parking area, a tricky scramble up a poison oak-laced road cut serves as the beginning of a steep dirt-and-brush march on a vague trail that leads to Snatch Power. An off-shoot just before this leads left and up for Finger Lickin'.

C **Finger Lickin' 5.10d** ★★ Pro: ¼ to 2½ inch. Continuous splitter. 5.10d can't get any harder.

D **Petty Larceny 5.11b** ★ Pro: Thin to 2 inch. Tough entry move to enjoyable jamming.

E **Snatch Power 5.10c** ★ Pro: Thin to 2 inch. Same as above.

F **Jaw Bone 5.10a** ★ Pro: 1 to 3 inch.

G **Pinky Paralysis 5.11c** ★★★ Pro: ¼ to 3 inch, especially ⅜ to 1¼ inch. Can be done in one pitch if one is mindful of rope drag early on. The name says it ... first and second knuckle finger-jamming.

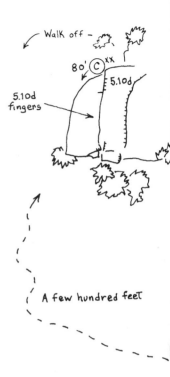

SHORT CIRCUIT BOULDER

This huge, split boulder lies on an island 0.1 mile up river from the Arch Rock parking area. The routes face down river.

A **666 5.12c** ★ Pro: QDs. Powerful bear-hugging with one really wicked section.

B **Short Circuit 5.11d** ★★ Pro: ⅜ to 1½ inch. Although usually toproped, this climb is sometimes soloed and rarely led. Slightly-overhanging, tight hand to finger-sized fracture. A must on the crack-climbing training circuit.

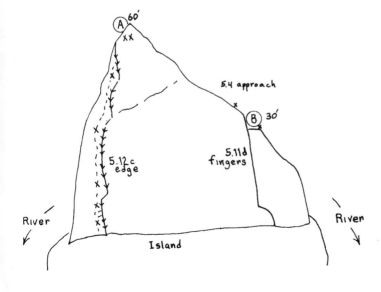

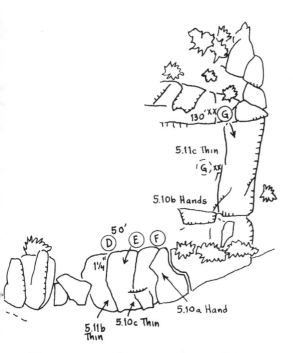

ROADSIDE ATTRACTION AREA

Parking for this area is located 3.5 miles west from the Hwy 120/140 intersection. A large boulder abutting a turnout on the side of the road and adjacent to the river is a convenient place to park.

H   **Roadside Attraction   5.12a**   ★★   Though usually toproped, this has been soloed once. Slightly overhanging. A leg pump then an arm pump.

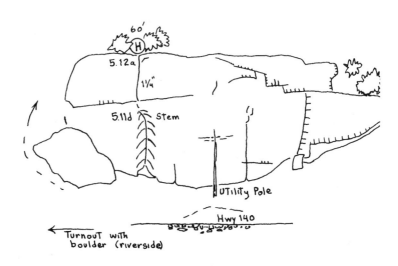

THE COOKIE CLIFF

Park at the turnout adjacent to the river (a half-mile down from the Cascade Falls Bridge) amid giant, white-talus boulders. Follow a climber's trail somewhat left of the talus field to meet the old road at the base of the cliff.

Descent. Contour left (down river). Near the margin of the cliff, angle down steep dirt, skirting short walls. One third-class move near the bottom of this section leads to the ground a short distance west of Tennessee Strings.

A **Tennessee Strings 5.12a** ★ Pro: Small to medium wireds, including HBs and TCUs. First knuckle cranks.

B **Hardd 5.11b** ★★★ Pro: ¼ to 3½ inch, especially ½ to 1½ inch pieces. First pitch: Staying fresh is helpful through the final moves. Second pitch: The finger crack is a bit harder than it first appears.

C **Crack-a-Go-Go 5.11c** ★★★ Pro: ¼ to 2 inch, especially ¼ to 1¼ inch. It is standard to rappel after the first pitch. Fine technique and using both cracks saves energy on this continuous pitch. Somewhat difficult to see the placements.

D **Outer Limits 5.10c** ★★★ Pro: ½ to 3½ inch, especially ¾ to 2½ inch. First pitch: This is strangely off-balance for a straight-in crack. Staying power is put to the test. Second pitch: Excellent hands to a boulder-type traverse. TCUs are helpful here.

E **The Cookie Monster 5.13b** ★★★ Pro: QDs. The route has been done free in one pitch, though when first freed it was done in two pitches. The first half involved lie-backing a shallow, arching crack. The second half cranks on flat edges up a wildly steep, orange wall.

F **Twilight Zone 5.10d** ★★ Pro to 6 inches.

G **Chips Ahoy 5.12c** ★ Pro: 10 QDs. Climb the right side of the arête.

H **Red Zinger 5.11d** ★★★ Pro to 2 inches. This route breaks away from, then comes close to rejoining Meat Grinder. First knuckle jams to a widening finger crack.

I **Meat Grinder 5.10c** ★★ Pro to 3½ inches. This follows the huge corner. Finish the second pitch by stepping into a belay alcove out left or continuing the off-width above to a belay, then a 5.8 hand pitch to get off.

J **Meat Grinder Arête 5.13b** ★★★ Pro: mostly QDs. A long pitch with slaps and dynos ... radical.

K **Beverly's Tower 5.10a** ★★ Pro: ¼ to 2½ inch, mainly small. Provides an easier way onto the Nabisco Wall.

L **Waverly Wafer 5.10c** ★★★ Pro: ½ to 2½ inch. A burning, 1¼ inch jam/lieback above the rest alcove.

M **Butterballs 5.11c** ★★★ Pro: ⅜ to 1¼ inch, with extra ¾ to 1¼ inch pieces. Continuous all-time finger crack.

N **Wheat Thin 5.10c** ★★★ Pro to 2 inches, especially ½ to 1¼ inch pieces. Move right, then an off-balance lieback gains a spectacular lieback flake. Very airy.

O **Butterfingers 5.11a** ★★ Pro: mainly ³⁄₁₆ to 1½ inch. A foothold appears as the crack diminishes. Then reach right—tight hands to the top.

P **Ladyfingers 5.11a** ★★ Pro: ¼ to 1½ inch. Move right from the belay, then follow discontinuous finger cracks up to a reach left—tight hands to the top.

Q **The Cookie—Right Side 5.9** ★★ Pro to 2½ inches. All there, but formidable nonetheless.

R **Anathema 5.10b** ★ (Only the first pitch is shown) Pro: ½ to 2½ inch. Leaning finger and hand jamming.

S **Catchy 5.10d** ★★★ Pro: ¼ to 2 inch. Span past a thin section at the top.

T **Catchy Corner 5.11a** ★★★ Pro to 2½ inches, with extra ½ to ¾ inch pieces. A thin layback section to a rest—endurance needed above.

Separate
Reality

The Cookie Cliff

COOKIE CLIFF

U **The Stigma (AKA Renegade) 5.13d** ★★ Pro: thin and high tech. Two bolts without hangers have been added. A pin-scarred, straight-in and slightly overhanging crack/seam.

V **The Enigma 5.10a** ★★ Pro to 2 ½ inches. Last pitches from left.
Regular 5.10a Last move is a lieback crux.
Ramp of Deception 5.10a Finger lock and lieback a steep ramp.
Abstract Corner 5.11d Bouldering or dynamic entry moves to finger jamming.

W **The Enema 5.11b** ★★★ Pro to 3 inches. A wildly overhanging hand crack, but then saddle a rest knob. Continue the flared vertical crack crux. Thin or fist jams.

THE COOKIE CLIFF

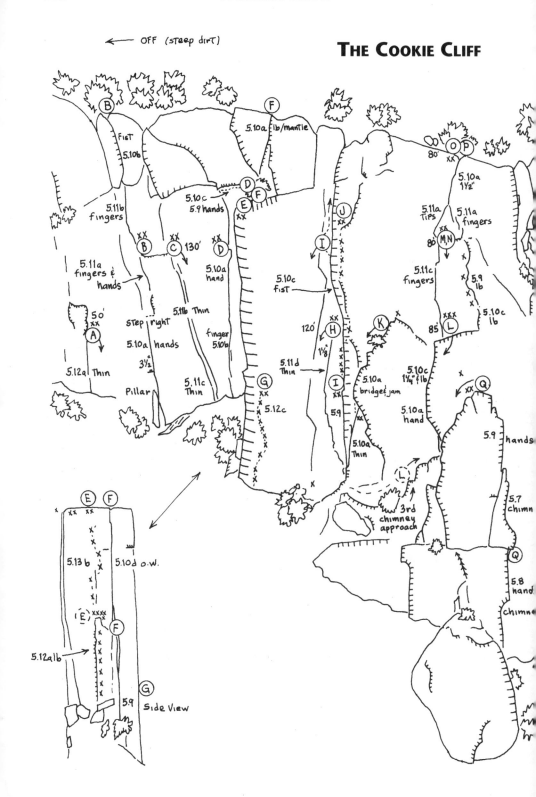

OFF (steep dirt)

Fist
5.10b

5.10a 11b/mantle

5.11b
fingers

5.10c
5.9 hands

80'

5.10a
1½"

5.11a
Tips

5.11a
fingers

80

5.11a
fingers & hands

130'

5.10a
hand

5.10c
fist

5.11c
fingers

5.9
1b

50'

5.11b Thin

Step right

finger
5.10b

120'

5.11d
Thin

85

5.10c
1b

5.12a Thin

5.10a hands

3½

5.11c
Thin

5.10a
bridge/jam

5.10c
1¼" & 1b

Pillar

5.11c
Thin

5.12c

5.9

5.10a
hand

5.9 hands

5.10a
Thin

3rd
chimney
approach

5.7
chimn

Side View

5.13 b

5.10d o.w.

5.12a 1b

5.9
Side View

5.8
hand

chimn

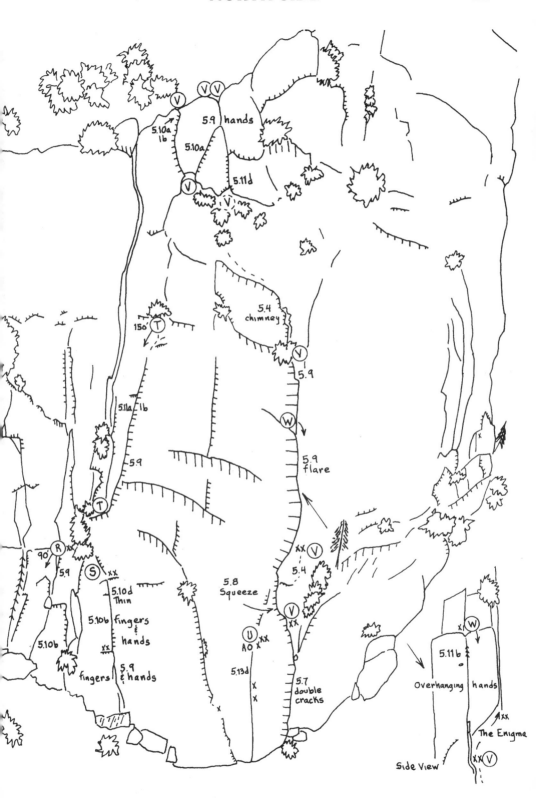

5.10a
1b

5.9 hands

5.10a

5.11d

5.4
chimney

150' Ⓣ

Ⓥ
5.9

5.11a 1b

Ⓦ

5.9
flare

5.9

Ⓣ

90' Ⓡ
xx

5.9   Ⓢ   xx

5.10d
Thin

5.10b   fingers
&
hands

5.10b

fingers   5.9
&hands

xx   Ⓥ
5.4

5.8
Squeeze

Ⓤ
AO   xx

5.13d

Ⓥ
xx

5.7
double
cracks

x
x

Ⓦ
5.11b

Overhanging hands

xx

The Enigma

Side View   xx Ⓥ

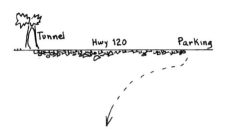

SEPARATE REALITY

From the eastern end of the longest tunnel on Hwy 120, scramble down brush and slabs to the edge.

A **Tales of Power 5.12b**
★★★ Pro: ¾ to 2½ inch, especially 1¼ to 1½ inches (also a fixed rappel line). Beautiful straight-in off-hand jamming on an overhanging wall.

B **Separate Reality 5.12a** ★★★ Pro: ¾ to 3½ inch, especially ½ to 3 inch (also a fixed rappel line). Airy roof from hand to fingers. At the lip, flip around.

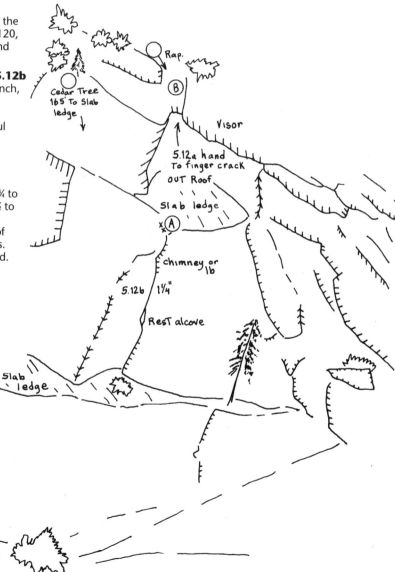

KNOBBY WALL

This incredibly steep boulder is located 20 yards to the north of Hwy 140 at 0.3 miles west of Cascade Creek Bridge and 0.4 miles east of the Cookie Cliff parking area.

This is sport-climbing central, and a guaranteed workout. Also, this area fosters a very different character from more traditional Yosemite climbing.

A **Portside (AKA Roland's Hole Route)   5.12b** ★★

B **Keep the Muscle, Lose the Fat   5.13b** ★★

C **The Flake   5.10b** ★★

D **Meltdown   5.12c** ★★

E **Changos Cabrones   5.12b** ★★

F **Unnamed   5.11b** ★★

G **Shaft of the Penetrator   5.12a** ★★

H **Unnamed   5.12a** ★★

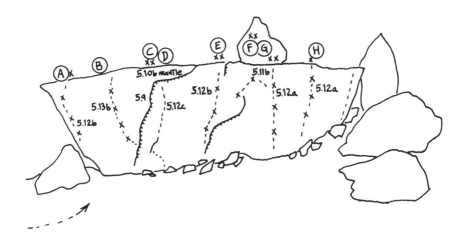

CASCADE AREA
1 **Sherrie's Crack   5.10c**
2 **The Tube   5.11a**
3 **Crimson Cringe   5.12a**
4 **The Phoenix   5.13a**

Sue McDevitt at the crux of Butterfingers, the Cookie Cliff
Walter J. Flint photo

PAT AND JACK PINNACLE AREA

A **Sherrie's Crack   5.10c** ★★   Pro: ⅜ to 2½ inch (TCUs). Finger cranks to enjoyable jamming.

B **Knob Job   5.10b** ★   Pro: ¼ to 3 inches. Crack switch and reach for jug.

C **Trough of Justice   5.10b** ★   Pro: QDs. Balance face and mantels on knobs—moves around arête.

D **Knuckleheads   5.10b** ★★

E **Desperado   5.11c** ★★   Pro: QDs (a few pieces optional). Power moves turning a roof.

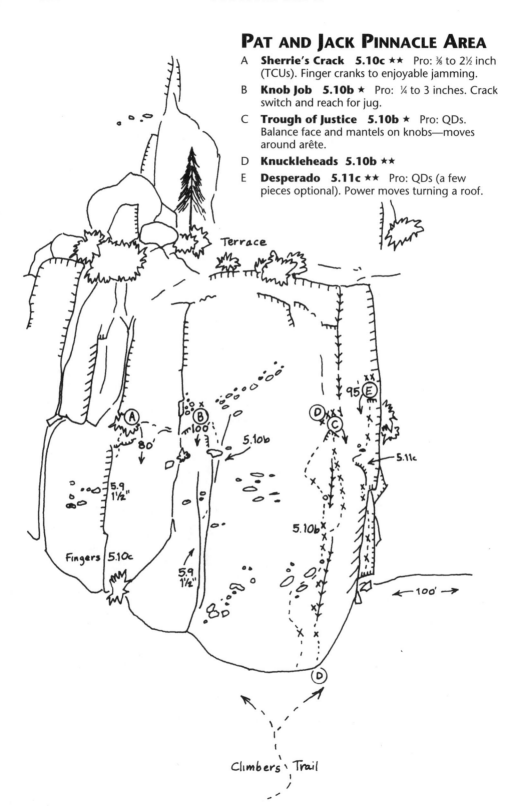

Pat and Jack Pinnacle Area

F **Skinheads 5.10d ★★★**

G **Underclingon 5.12a ★★** Pro: QDs (piece up high optional). Delicate endurance arch. An interesting face above.

H **The Tube 5.11a ★★★** Pro: ⅛ to 2½ inches. Appealing corner with abstract lieback and wedging at the crux.

I **Polymastia 5.10d ★** Pro: QDs and a few 1 to 2 inch pieces for the inital crack section. Balance and sequence are key.

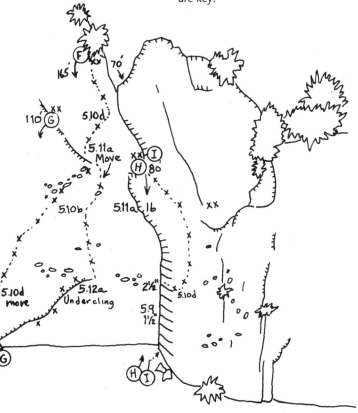

CASCADE FALLS

These climbs are located on the wall left of Cascade Falls. Park in the large turnout immediately west of Cascade Creek Bridge on Hwy 140. Hike up the creek bed. Starting these climbs will be difficult during periods of high water.

A **Fish Crack 5.12b** ★★ Pro: Wireds and .4 to 1.5 TCUs; also, one 3½ inch piece for the start. Slightly flared fingers.

B **Free Press 5.10a** ★★ Pro to 3½ inch. One grunt section—use your fingers in the back of a body-sized flare.

C **Crimson Cringe 5.12a** ★★★ Pro: ½ to 3 inch wireds, with extra 1¼ to 2 inch pieces. Cranking reaches to solid fingers, continuing to off-hand endurance climbing. Finally, sporty moves take you out a lieback/undercling.

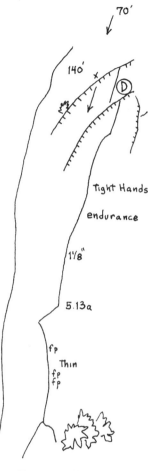

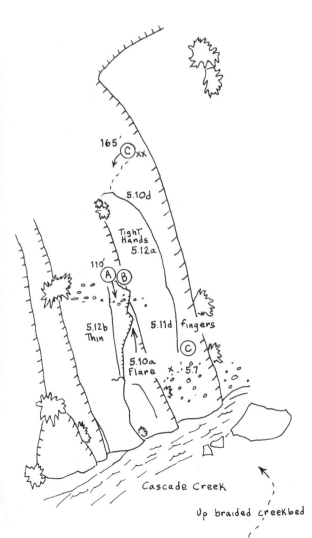

CASCADE FALLS—UPPER

Phoenix is located on the upper west side of Cascade Falls. It is approached from above via Hwy 120 and two rappels. From the west end of the Tamarack Creek bridge (2 miles west of the Hwy 120/140 junction), walk down to an open, flat area. Cross the brook and contour to the brink of the trees, where you'll find a one-bolt, two-piton station. From here, a 140-foot rappel leads to the bottom of the crack.

D **The Phoenix 5.13a** ★★★ Pro: Small to 2¼ inch. This is an incredible splitter.

KNOB HILL

This bluff is located above Hwy 120, immediately to the east of Cascade Creek. Park across the road in a paved parking area and scramble steeply up and right to the base of the cliff.

Descent. Scramble off the top of Knob Hill to the west, encountering steep and dirty third-class chimneys and gullies.

This is a good beginner's area, except perhaps for the descent which can be mitigated by a rappel.

E **Pot Belly 5.7** ★ Pro to 2 inches, especially ½ to 1¼ inch pieces.

F **Movin' To Montana 5.8** ★

G **Sloth Wall 5.7** ★ Pro to 2½ inches.

H **Anti-Ego Crack 5.7** ★ Pro to 2½ inches.

I **Turkey Pie (AKA Chicken Pie)**
5.7 ★ Pro to 2½ inches.

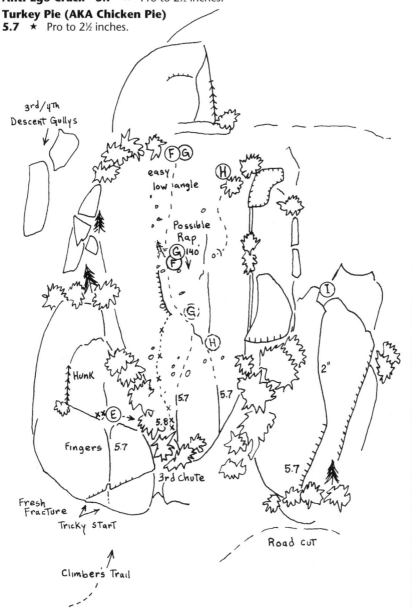

KNOB HILL

Hwy 120

THIS AND THAT CLIFF

LOWER MERCED CANYON
1 Cramming
2 Scram

3 The Iota
4 Reed Pinnacle
5 Lunatic Fringe
6 Stone Groove

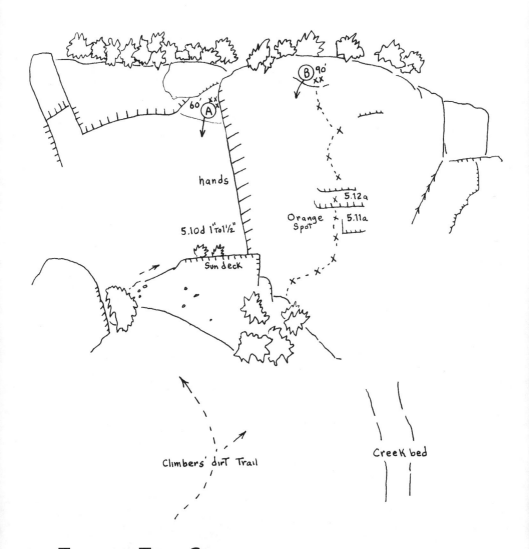

THIS AND THAT CLIFF

Park on Hwy 140 at a point approximately 1.5 miles down and west of the Hwy 120/140 junction. Hike up a vague climber's trail on the eastern (right) section of this long cliff. A good starting point lies between the two easternmost of a group of houses in the area.

A **Cramming 5.10d** ★★★   Pro: ¾ to 2½ inch, especially ¾ to 1½ inch pieces. A short yet appealing fracture, conducive to doing laps. It is warm in winter.

B **Scram 5.12a** ★★★   Pro: QDs. Great rock with one hard pull getting over the roof.

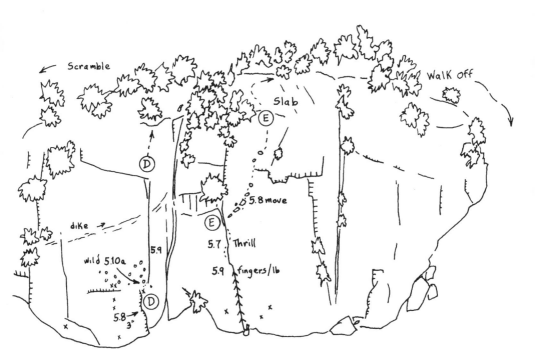

New Diversions Cliff

Park near the old generator station off Hwy 140, 1.2 miles west of the Hwy 120/140 junction. A climber's trail starts up the hill a hundred feet or so east (up river) from the station.

C **New Diversions 5.10a** ★★★ Pro to 3¼ inches, including long runners (knob tie-offs). This is hair-raising, featuring big knobs on a steep wall.

D **Chicken Pie 5.9** ★★ Pro to 2½ inches, especially ½ to 1¾ inch pieces (optional: pieces to 3½ inches and knob tie-offs).

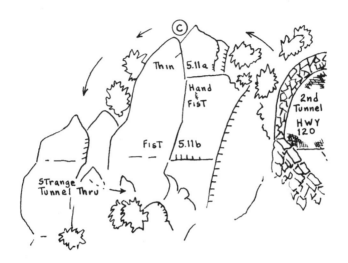

GOLDRUSH AREA

Park at Reed's Pinnacle Area (the turnout between the two short tunnels on Hwy 120). Goldrush easily is seen as the crack immediately left of the westernmost tunnel. From the area atop Goldrush, drop down a strange tunnel through blocks to reach the start of the climb.

A   **Goldrush 5.11b** ★ Pro: Small to 3¾ inch, especially 2½ to 3½ inch pieces. This is a slightly overhanging, leaning, burly fist crack.

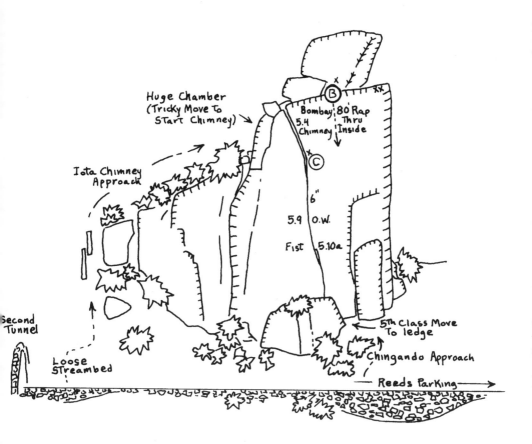

Huge Chamber
(Tricky Move to
Start Chimney)

Iota Chimney
Approach

Bombay 80' Rap
5.4 Thru
Chimney Inside

6"

5.9 O.W.

Fist 5.10a

5th Class Move
To ledge

Chingando Approach

Second
Tunnel

Loose
Streambed

Reeds Parking

REED'S PINNACLE AREA
FAR LEFT—IOTA

B **The Iota 5.6** ★ Pro: A few nuts are optional. High Indiana Jones-value for a short climb.

C **Chingando 5.10a** ★ Pro: 2 to 6 inches. Part of the Hardman Offwidth Training Circuit.

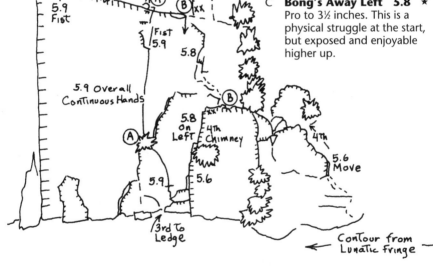

In The Corner
5.9
O.W.

5.9
finger
&
Hand

(B) 80'
x

5.5

5.8 Fist

(C) x
xx

100'

(B)

5.6 Tunnel Thru
Squeeze

5.9
Fist

(A)(A) 165'
(B) xx

Fist
5.9

5.8

5.9 Overall
Continuous Hands

(A)

5.8
on
Left

4th
Chimney

(B)
xx

5.9

5.6

4th

5.6
Move

3rd To
Ledge

Contour from
Lunatic fringe

REED'S PINNACLE AREA—LEFT

A **Reed's Direct 5.9 ★★★**
(first two pitches only.)   Pro to 3½ inch (nuts useful). A truly classic jamming exercise. A short warm-up pitch to endurance hand-slamming on the second pitch. One 165-foot rap will just make ledges.

B **Reed's Regular Route 5.9**
★★★ Pro to 3½ inches. There are many first-pitch variations. Adventuresome tunnel-thru to a choice of cracks up the summit block.

C **Bong's Away Left 5.8 ★**
Pro to 3½ inches. This is a physical struggle at the start, but exposed and enjoyable higher up.

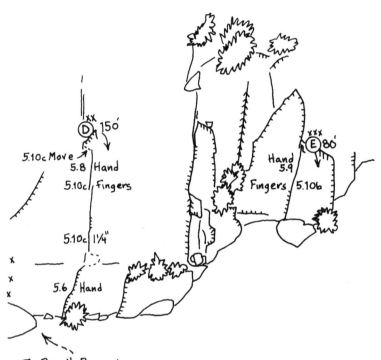

150'

D

XX

5.10c Move

5.8 Hand

5.10c Fingers

5.10c 1¼"

5.6 Hand

Hand
5.9

Fingers 5.10b

E 80'
XXX

To Reed's Pinnacle

From low point in roadcut
Just West of Turnout

REED'S PINNACLE AREA—RIGHT

D **Lunatic Fringe 5.10c** ★★★ Pro: ¼ to 2½ inches (especially ¾ to 2 inch pieces). Short warm-up to varied straight-in jamming on a steep white wall.

E **Stone Groove 5.10b** ★★ Pro: ⅜ to 2½ inch (especially ¾ to 1½ inch pieces). Cranker finger/tight hands to crux 30 feet up.

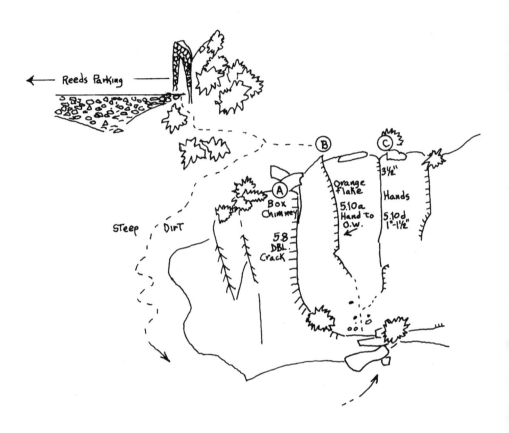

FIVE AND DIME CLIFF

A **Keystone Corner   5.8**   ★   Pro to 2½ inch.
Jamming and stemming in a steep corner.

B **Copper Penny   5.10a**   ★   Pro to 6 inches.
The crux is the entry to the offwidth. Inside
edge for long arms—steep and wild.

C **Five and Dime   5.10d**   ★★★   Pro to 2½
inch. Slightly overhanging, straight-in, a range
of sizes. Beautiful.

HWY STAR BLUFF

This bluff is unseen from the road, yet only two
minutes away. Park at the first large dirt turnout east
of the Hwy 120/140 junction. A 25 mph sign is a
useful marker for the start of the uphill hike.

D **Highway Star 5.10a ★** Pro ¾ to 2½ inch.
Steep hand jamming—great for doing laps.

Walter Flint on the last pitch of The Nose.
Dave Schultz photo, Walter J. Flint collection

EL CAPITAN

Park 0.1 miles west of the El Capitan Bridge. Take the climber's trail that heads back through the woods directly toward The Nose. Beneath that route, the trail divides, leading along both sides of the cliff.

Negative Pinnacle is just a short distance along the southeast face or the branch of trail heading right. By continuing along, the East Buttress eventually is reached. A more direct approach, however, ascends talus directly above a picnic pullout 2.1 miles west of the gas station.

For the other routes, proceed along the southwest face or left branch of the trail. All but the Salathé and West Face climb to exfoliated "summits" that sit just above the base of El Capitan. The first route you'll encounter walking up from The Nose is Pine Line, followed by the Salathé Wall, Moby Dick, Little John, La Cosita, The Slack and La Escuela, as well as others not listed in this guide.

The West Face lies well above. The scruffy barrier surrounding the West Buttress is negotiated by dropping down and around the corner to a third-class path that leads up. To proceed further up, the main chimney/drainage (the West Chimney) must be skirted to the left on a third-class rib, until you are above the chockstone.

DESCENT   Most climbers descent from the top of El Cap to the valley floor by one of the following ways: 1. Hike up several hundred yards to the rounded summit knoll, and pick up the trail that heads back into the woods. The campground off the Tuolomne road at Tamarack Flat can be reached after about eight miles of rolling but mostly gentle downhill hiking. Consult a map. 2. From the woods behind El Cap, a trail can be taken east along the rim past Eagle Peak to the Yosemite Falls Trial for a descent directly to Camp 4. The Falls Trail section of this eight-mile descent is grueling in its continuous steepness. 3. The East Ledges descent requires some third-class scrambling and some rappels, but does offer the advantages of being snow-free in the early season—not to mention, it's only about two hours to the valley floor.

The
West Face
Route

EL CAPITAN—WEST FACE

EL CAPITAN—WEST FACE

VI 5.11c ★★ Pro: Tiny high tech to 3½ inch. Quick parties currently do the route in a day. Climbers also can approach, fix two pitches and sleep at the base, then complete the climb.

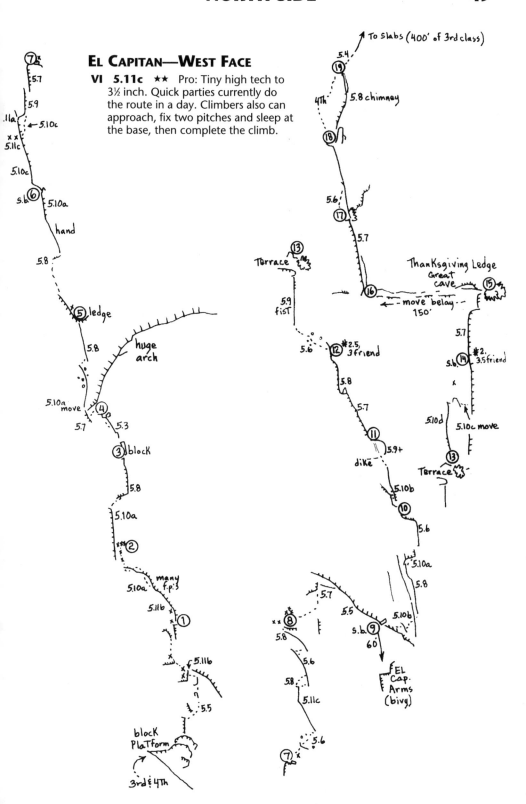

EL CAPITAN—BASE ROUTES

A   **La Escuela 5.11b ★★★** Pro:
Many small pieces to 2½ inch.

B   **Sacherer Cracker to The Slack
5.10 a ★★★** Pro to 3½ inch.
Most parties rappel after the first
pitch. Higher up, you'll enter the
bowels of El Cap. The anchor on
the summit could use some
reinforcement.

C   **The Mark of Art 5.10d ★★**
Pro to 2½ inch, with extra ¾ to 1½
inch pieces.

D   **Short but Thin 5.11b ★**
Pro: Small. This is most often
toproped.

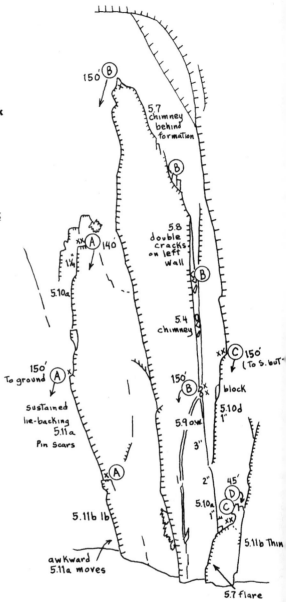

EL CAPITAN—BASE ROUTES

E **La Cosita (Left Side Variation)** **5.9** ★ Spooky.

La Cosita (Left Side) **5.7** ★★★ Pro to 2½ inch. Steep, wild and improbable for 5.7. Be creative.

F **La Cosita (Right Side)** **5.9** ★★★ Pro to 2¼ inch, especially ⅜ to 1½ inch pieces. Smooth, thin jams and liebacks.

G **Little John (Left Side)** **5.8** ★ Pro to 3½ inch. Robust and smooth.

H **Little John (Right Side)** **5.8** ★★ Pro from ¼ to 3 inch. A stiff adventure over three pitches.

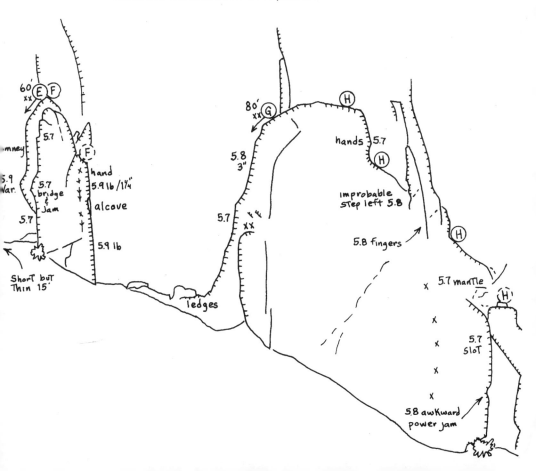

El Capitan—Moby Dick

A   **Moby Dick (Center)**   **5.10a**   ★★★   Pro to 3½ inch, especially 2 to 3 inch pieces. Torturous finger locks to start. Physically sustained jamming above.

B   **Moby Dick (Ahab)**   **5.10b**   ★   Pro to 3 inch. V-shaped, leaning slot . . . a struggle for security and upward progress.

C   **Pine Line**   **5.7**   ★★   Pro from ¼ to 1½ inch.

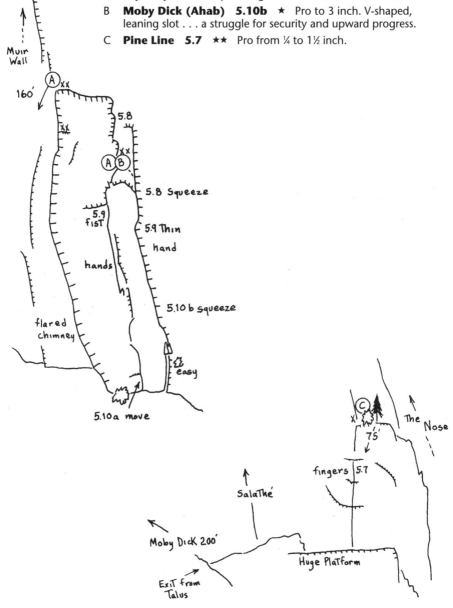

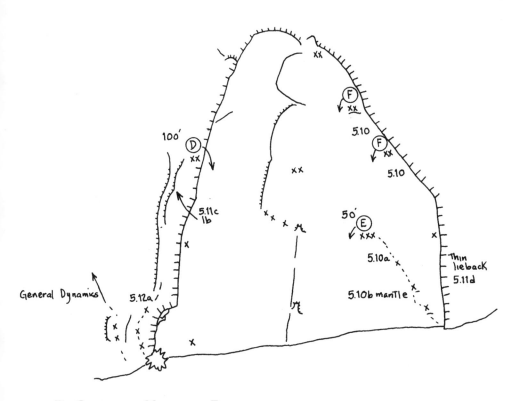

EL CAPITAN—NEGATIVE PINNACLE

D **Base Hits 5.12a** ★ Pro: Small to 1½ inch.

E **Party Mix 5.10b** ★ Pro: Three QDs. Quality rock with fair-sized holds.
A steep balance challenge.

F **The High Arc 5.11d** ★ Pro: Bring many tiny pieces.

West Face
Approach

EL CAPITAN—SOUTHWEST FACE

1 La Escuela	4 Little John	7 Pine Line
2 The Slack	5 Moby Dick	8 The Nose
3 La Cosita	6 Salathé Wall	

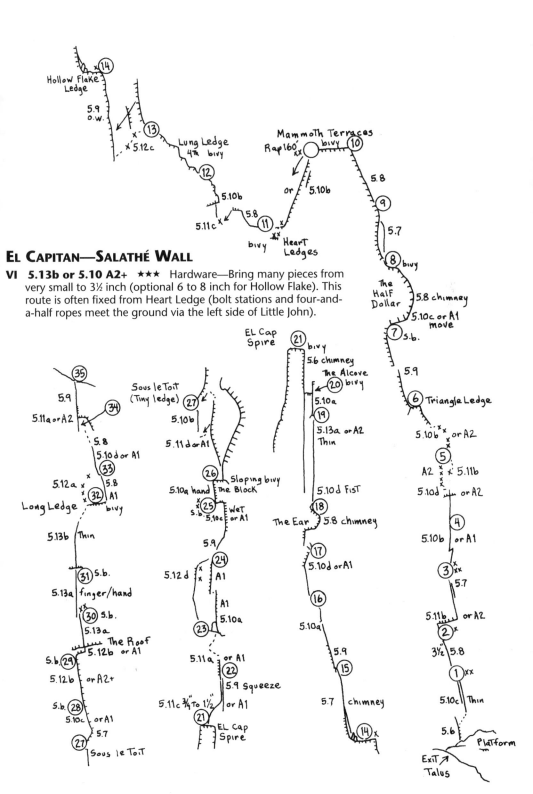

EL CAPITAN—SALATHÉ WALL

VI 5.13b or 5.10 A2+ ★★★ Hardware—Bring many pieces from very small to 3½ inch (optional 6 to 8 inch for Hollow Flake). This route is often fixed from Heart Ledge (bolt stations and four-and-a-half ropes meet the ground via the left side of Little John).

EL CAPITAN— THE NOSE

VI 5.13b or 5.11 A2 ★★★

Hardware—Bring wireds, Friends (two each) to #4, nuts to 3½ inch. Parties often fix to Sickle Ledge. Speed ascents often work different strategies with regard to maximum pitch height and belay locations.

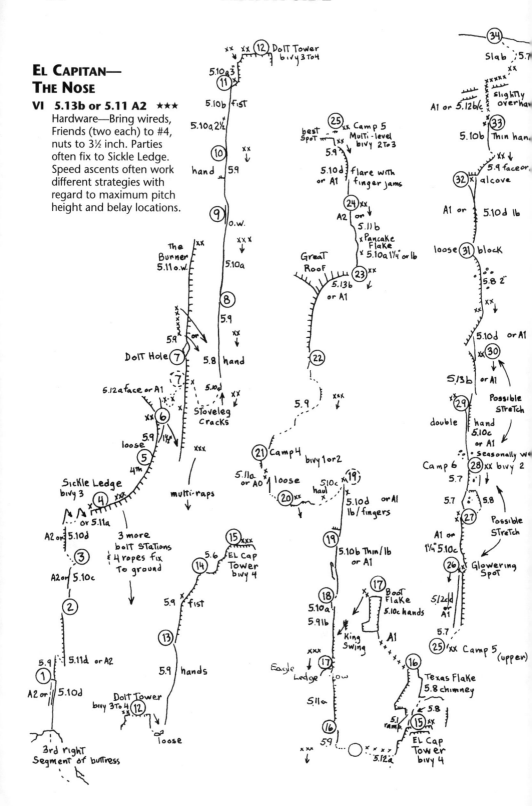

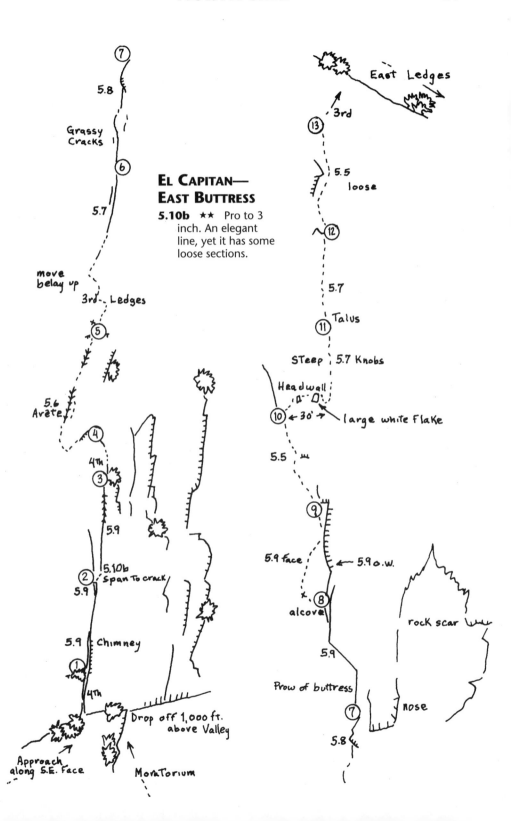

**EL CAPITAN—
EAST BUTTRESS**

5.10b ★★ Pro to 3 inch. An elegant line, yet it has some loose sections.

East Ledges

3rd

5.5 loose

5.7 Talus

Steep 5.7 Knobs

Headwall

large white Flake

← 30' →

5.5

5.8

Grassy Cracks

5.7

move belay up

3rd Ledges

5.6 Arête

4TH

5.9

5.10b Span To crack

5.9

5.9 Chimney

4TH

Drop off 1,000 ft. above Valley

Approach along S.E. Face

MoraTorium

5.9 Face ← 5.9 o.w.

alcove

5.9

Prow of buttress

rock scar

Nose

5.8

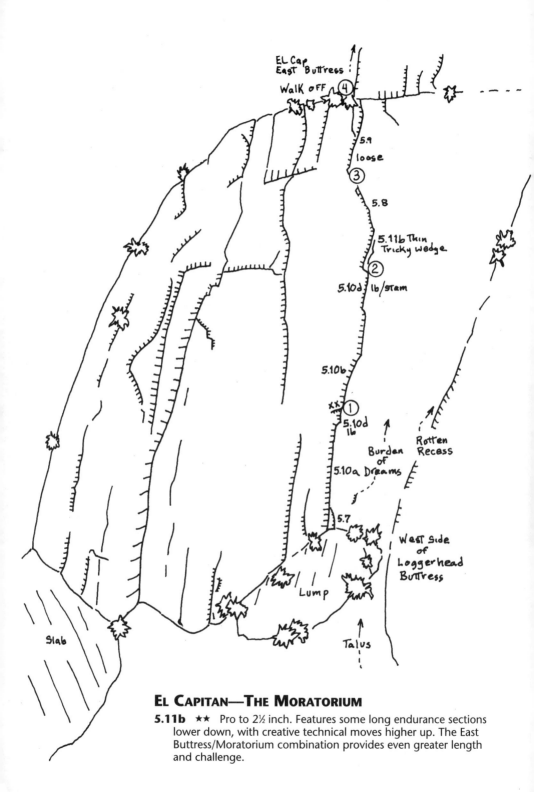

EL Cap
East Buttress
Walk off ④

5.9
loose
③

5.8

5.11b Thin
Tricky Wedge
②

5.10d lb/stem

5.10b

xx ①
5.10d
lb

Burden
of
5.10a Dreams

Rotten
Recess

5.7

West Side
of
Loggerhead
Buttress

Lump

Talus

Slab

El Capitan—The Moratorium

5.11b ★★ Pro to 2½ inch. Features some long endurance sections
lower down, with creative technical moves higher up. The East
Buttress/Moratorium combination provides even greater length
and challenge.

EL CAP EAST LEDGE/EAGLE CREEK

1 **East Buttress**
2 **The Moratorium**
3 **Slab Happy Pinnacle**
4 **East Ledge Descent**
5 **After Six**
6 **The Nutcracker**

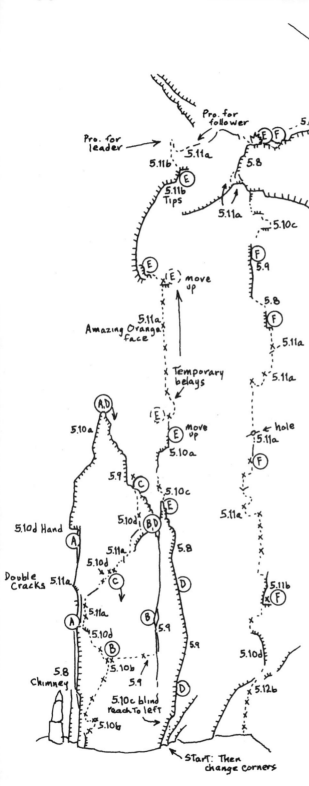

EL CAPITAN— SLAB HAPPY PINNACLE

Park in the dirt turnout 1.7 miles west of the gas station and 0.2 mile past the El Cap Picnic Area. Hike up the hill, skirting the east side of Loggerhead Buttress. Traverse right along a barrier until third-class passage can be made to the main wall. Slab Happy is out to the left along a broad ledge system. Nearby Horsetail Fall and afternoon winds can affect climbing conditions in this area.

A   **Left Side 5.11a** ★
Pro to 3 inch.

B   **Center Route 5.10b** ★
Pro to 3½ inch.

C   **The Happy Ending 5.11a** ★   Pro to 2½ inch.

D   **The Dihardral 5.10c** ★
Pro to 3 inch.

E   **Never Say Dog 5.11b** ★★ Pro to 3 inch with extra pieces to 2 inch. Bold and beautiful.

F   **The Big Juan 5.12b** ★★ Pro: Many to 2 inch. Also bold and beautiful.

EL CAPITAN—EAST LEDGES DESCENT

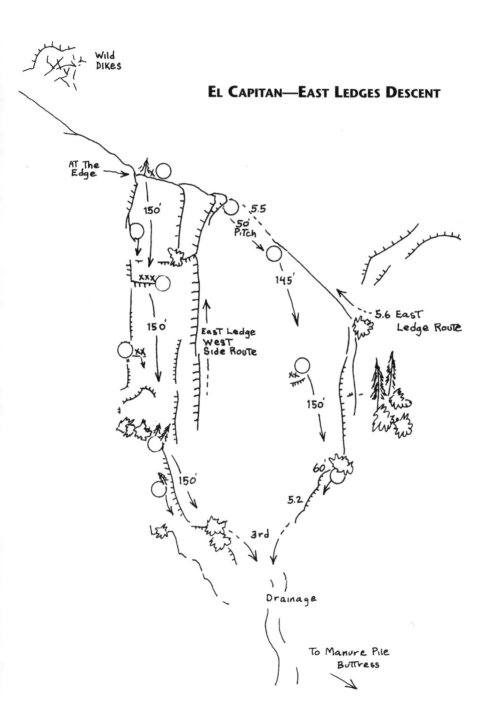

Wild Dikes

AT The Edge

150'

.5.5

50' Pitch

145'

xxx

150'

East Ledge West Side Route

5.6 East Ledge Route

xx

150'

xx

150'

150'

60'

5.2

3rd

Drainage

To Manure Pile Buttress

MANURE PILE BUTTRESS

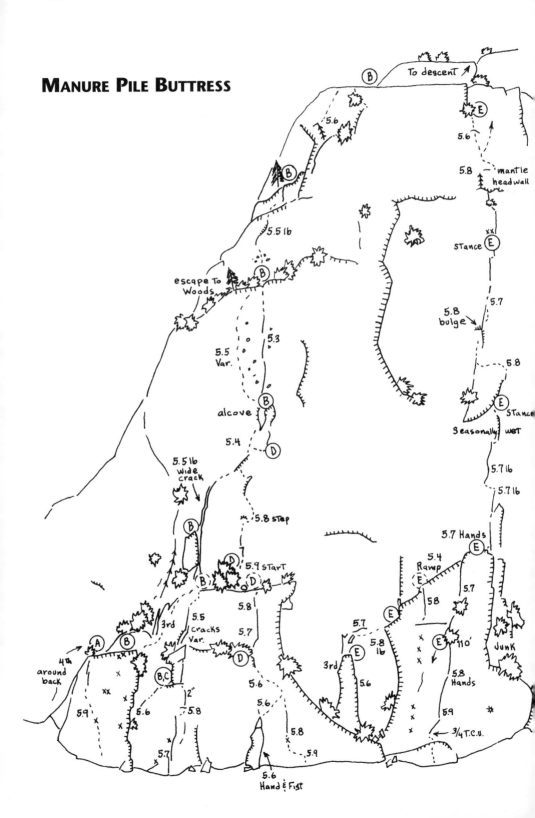

MANURE PILE BUTTRESS

Park at the El Cap Picnic area, 1.6 miles west of the gas station. Walk the closed dirt road on the north side of the highway to the formation.

DESCENT   Scramble off the top of the formation to the west to gain a steep, dirty gully.

A **Jump for Joy 5.9 ★** Pro: A few pieces to 2 inch. Reachy moves up and left to slick, positive edges allows escape from the initial bowl/depression.

B **After Six 5.6 ★★** Pro to 2½ inch. The crux is found on the first pitch and many parties escape after that. Moderate to easy climbing with big ledges and superior views are found above.

C **After Seven 5.8 ★** Pro to 2½ inch. Jamming leads to face moves that are not obvious. The face moves lead right, then up.

D **C.S. Concerto 5.9 ★** Pro to 2½ inch. Varied climbing that is somewhat runout on the first and third pitches.

E **Nutcracker 5.8 ★★★** Pro to 2½ inch, especially small to medium pieces. Intriguing climbing, clean rock. A number of starting variations exist.

THE FOLLY

From a point 0.4 mile west of the gas station, hike to the wall, then up and right to these routes.

A **Childhood's End 5.11a** ★★ Pro to 3 inch, especially 1 to 2½ inch pieces. Generally solid jams in the back of flared, leaning corners.

B **Follywood 5.12c** ★★ Pro to 2½ inches. Continuous finger stuff and liebacks.

C **The Good Book (AKA Right Side of The Folly) 5.10d** ★★★ Pro to 3 inch. Perhaps the best Yosemite crack climb of its grade. Steep, clean and sustained crack climbing.

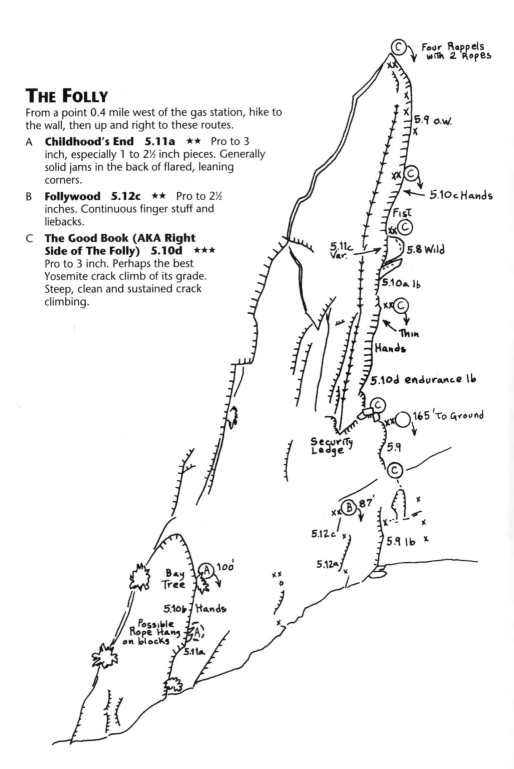

Four Rappels with 2 Ropes

5.9 o.w.

5.10c Hands

Fist

5.8 Wild

5.11c Var.

5.10a lb

Thin

Hands

5.10d endurance lb

165' To Ground

Security Ledge

5.9

87'

5.12c

5.9 lb

5.12a

Bay Tree

100'

5.10b Hands

Possible Rope Hang on blocks

5.11a

EL CAPITAN

LOWER BROTHER

1

3

2

4

5

CAMP 4 WALLS

LOWER BROTHER

1 **Manure Pile Buttress**
2 **Childhood's End**
3 **The Folly**
4 **Doggie Deviations**
5 **Henley Quits**

CAMP 4 WALL

Hike up the stream bed that meets the west end of Camp 4.

A   **Doggie Diversions**   **5.9**   ★   Pro to 3½ inches with extra 2 to 3½ inch pieces. Most parties do one pitch.

B   **Doggie Deviations**   **5.9**   ★★   Pro to 2½ inches. Fairly straightforward and enjoyable.
Flake Variation   5.9   ★★   Pro to 2½ inch. Only slightly expanding. Gratifying moves.

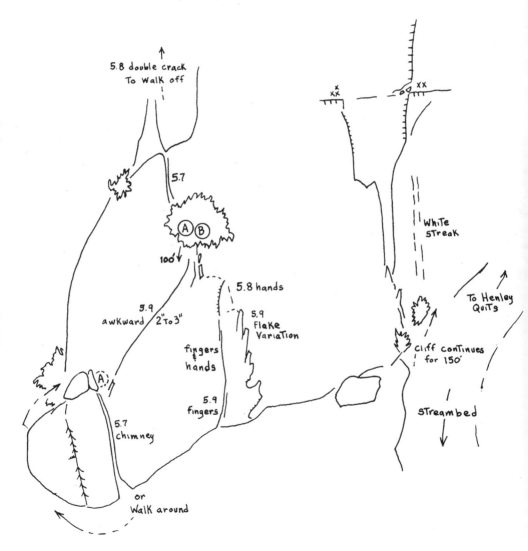

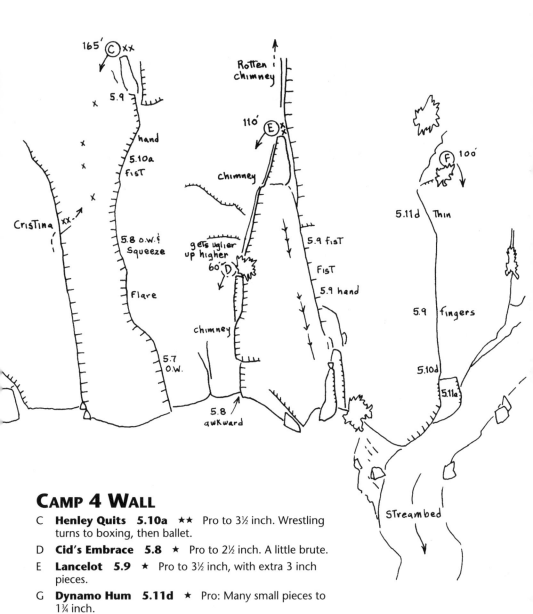

165' C xx
5.9
hand
5.10a
fist
CrisTina xx
5.8 o.w. &
Squeeze
Flare
5.7
O.W.

Rotten
chimney
110'
E x
x
chimney
gets uglier
up higher
60' D
chimney
5.8
awkward
5.9 fist
Fist
5.9 hand

F 100'
5.11d Thin
5.9 fingers
5.10d
5.11a
STreambed

CAMP 4 WALL

C **Henley Quits 5.10a** ★★ Pro to 3½ inch. Wrestling
turns to boxing, then ballet.

D **Cid's Embrace 5.8** ★ Pro to 2½ inch. A little brute.

E **Lancelot 5.9** ★ Pro to 3½ inch, with extra 3 inch
pieces.

G **Dynamo Hum 5.11d** ★ Pro: Many small pieces to
1¾ inch.

Upper Yosemite Falls Trail

LOWER YOSEMITE FALLS AREA

1 **Munginella**
2 **Commitment**
3 **Ten Years After**
4 **Mean Streak**

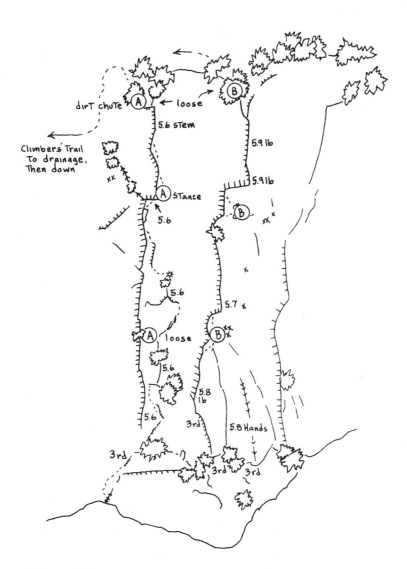

FIVE OPEN BOOKS

These climbs can be reached from a faint trail that leads up and left from the left side of the bridge at the base of Lower Yosemite Falls. A shorter, but less obvious way is to hike up, leaving the Lower Yosemite Falls Trail just before encountering a boulder field on the left. Descent. Scramble down the drainage to the west.

A **Munginella 5.6** ★★ Pro to 2½ inch. Provides a spectrum of 5.6 challenges over three pitches.

B **Commitment 5.9** ★★ Pro to 3 inch, especially ½ to 2 inch pieces. Turns a dramatic roof on the final pitch.

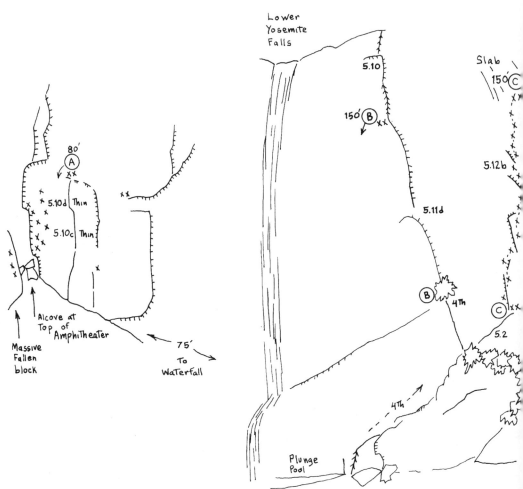

LOWER YOSEMITE FALLS

These climbs are on the right side of the Lower Yosemite Falls amphitheater. They are climbable only during periods of lower water.

A **Ten Years After 5.10d** ★★★ Pro: ⅛ to 2 inch, especially medium wireds. Good finger locks or hand jams are never more than a move away, yet this climb is very sustained.

B **Fight or Flight 5.11d** ★★ Pro: Medium wireds and Friends to #2½ (two each) and #3, #3½ Friends (one each).

C **Mean Streak 5.12b** ★★ Pro: Extra long QDs and runners to avoid rope drag. This climb involves cranking on a tiger-striped wall. It has a crowd-pleasing location.

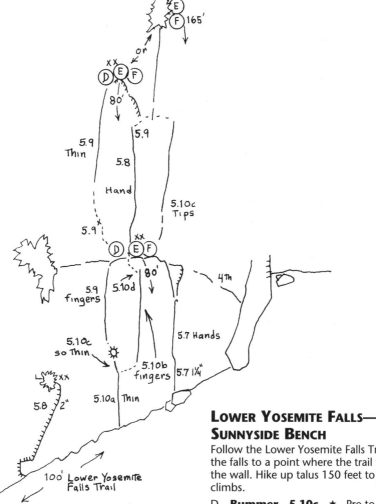

LOWER YOSEMITE FALLS— SUNNYSIDE BENCH

Follow the Lower Yosemite Falls Trail past the falls to a point where the trail touches the wall. Hike up talus 150 feet to these climbs.

D **Bummer 5.10c** ★ Pro to 2 inch, especially tiny to 1 inch pieces. A frustrating move gains a small crystal hole. A little spooky to clip the bolt on the second pitch and somewhat vegged.

E **Lazy Bum 5.10d** ★★ Pro to 2 inch, especially tiny to 1 inch pieces. Most parties do only the first pitch, which thins and forces moves out left to a distant edge.

F **Jamcrack Route 5.9** ★★ Pro to 2 inch. Both pitches yield excellent straight-in finger and hand jamming.

UPPER YOSEMITE FALLS

Crux of the Arrow Tip

Walter J. Flint photo

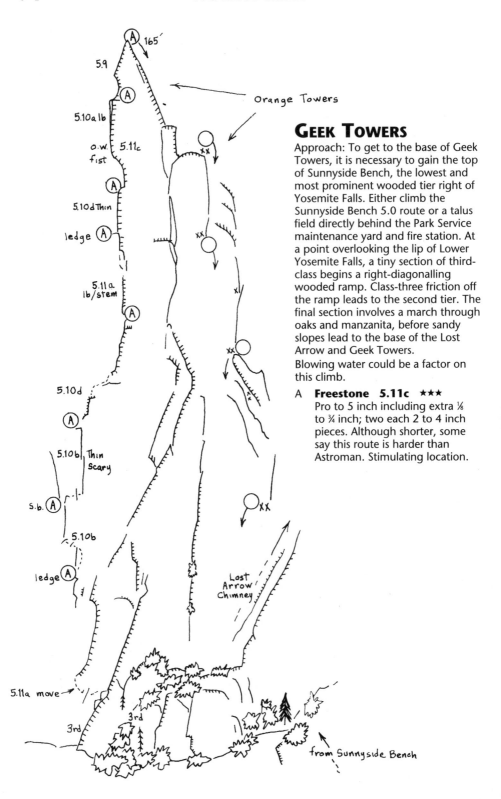

165'

5.9

5.10a lb

o.w. 5.11c
fist

5.10d Thin

ledge

5.11a
lb/stem

5.10d

5.10b Thin
Scary

s.b.

5.10b

ledge

5.11a move

3rd

3rd

Orange Towers

GEEK TOWERS

Approach: To get to the base of Geek Towers, it is necessary to gain the top of Sunnyside Bench, the lowest and most prominent wooded tier right of Yosemite Falls. Either climb the Sunnyside Bench 5.0 route or a talus field directly behind the Park Service maintenance yard and fire station. At a point overlooking the lip of Lower Yosemite Falls, a tiny section of third-class begins a right-diagonalling wooded ramp. Class-three friction off the ramp leads to the second tier. The final section involves a march through oaks and manzanita, before sandy slopes lead to the base of the Lost Arrow and Geek Towers.

Blowing water could be a factor on this climb.

A **Freestone 5.11c** ★★★
Pro to 5 inch including extra ⅛ to ¾ inch; two each 2 to 4 inch pieces. Although shorter, some say this route is harder than Astroman. Stimulating location.

Lost
Arrow
Chimney

from Sunnyside Bench

Lost Arrow Spire

This route starts by rappelling from the rim of the valley, near Yosemite Point, into the notch behind the spire. Two ropes needed to be fixed for the return to the rim.

One method is to rappel the climbing route, then ascend the fixed ropes back to the rim. A two-bolt station will be found at the 150 foot interval.

The other method is a Tyrolean Traverse. Two 'fix' ropes are joined, and one end is then anchored to the rim. This requires that the knot joining the ropes be safely passed during the rappel into the notch. The bottom, free end of the fixed ropes is then towed along while climbing.

This is a very spectacular setting. Except for the section leading to Salathé Ledge, the route is almost entirely fixed.

B **Lost Arrow Tip   5.12b or   5.8/5.10a A2   ★★**   Pro:
A few pieces, especially 2½ to 3½ inch for the upper part of the first pitch. A few rivet hangers/tie-off loops and many carabiners are also needed.

Yosemite Point
railing 300'

Pine Tree

Rim

275'
To notch

Horn

alcove

5.12b

165' Pitch
use many
runners

Belay here
for
low rope drag
free climbing

Salathé Ledge

5.9
3"to4"

5.10a
Fist

Notch

5.10d
pin scars

Second Terror

CHURCH BOWL

Generous turnouts on the road just east of the village and medical clinic lie beneath the cliff.

A **Uncle Fanny** **5.7** ★ Pro to 2 inches. A prelude to a valley of demanding cracks.

B **Church Bowl Lieback** **5.8** ★ Pro to 2 inch, especially ¼ to 1 inch pieces. An overlooked, semi-precious stone.

C **Pole Position** **5.10a** ★ Pro: QDs. A bit of a squeeze job, but pleasant climbing.

D **Revival** **5.10a** ★ Pro: Small to 2 inch. Possible missing bolt hanger.

E **Aunt Fanny's Pantry** **5.4** ★ Pro to 2 inches. Ungraceful moves down low, yet a good beginner climb. Rappel the route from bolts on a perch straight down, or tunnel behind the pillar and down a bit. A short rappel from trees leads to Church Bowl Terrace. Another short rappel from bolts on the edge of the ledge ends at the ground.

F **Book of Revelations** **5.11a** ★★ Pro: Many small to 2 inches. Tough moves interspersed with awkward rests on the first pitch. On the second pitch, change cracks by moving right to meet a thin finger crack, crank crux. The climb continues, but most parties do just two pitches.

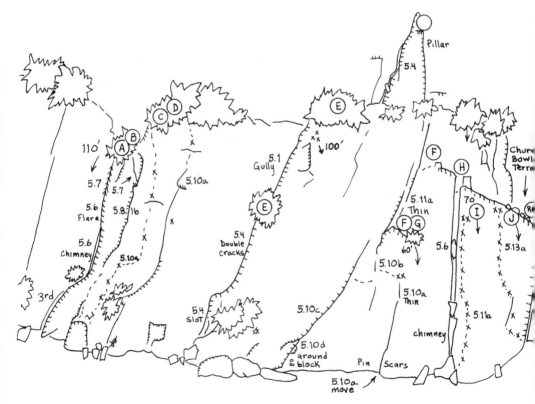

G **Church Bowl Tree** **5.10b** ★★ Pro: Mainly small to 1½ inches. One of the greasiest climbs in the valley. Balancey stand-up moves on fair holds, passing a pair of bolts.

H **Church Bowl Chimney** **5.6** ★ Pro to 2 ½ inches. Physical and sometimes humbling.

I **The Energizer** **5.11a** ★★ Pro: Nine QDs. Starts on the right side of an arête. Hard not to stand on the tree midway.

J **Atheist** **5.13a** ★★ Pro: TCUs and nine QDs. A long reach and cranking skills are necessary. Short-armed vandals stole the hangers off the first two bolts.

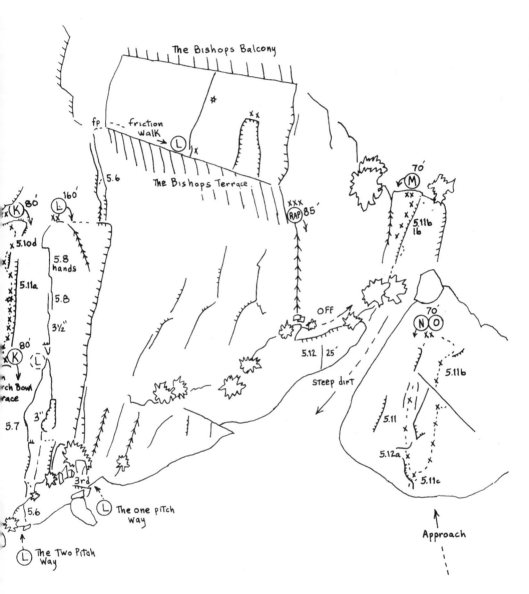

K **Bitches' Terror 5.11a** ★★ Pro: Many QDs. Keen climbing on a blunt arête.

L **Bishop's Terrace 5.8** ★★★ Pro to 3½ inches. This classic test piece of 5.8 jamming leads to a novel location.

M **No Rest for the Wicked 5.11b** ★ Pro: A few wireds, #1½ and #2 Friends and QDs. This is an off-balance lieback.

N **Oral Roberts 5.12a** ★★ Pro: QDs and a few pieces to 2½ inch.

O **700 Club 5.11c** ★★ Pro: Seven QDs, wired or small TCU optional.

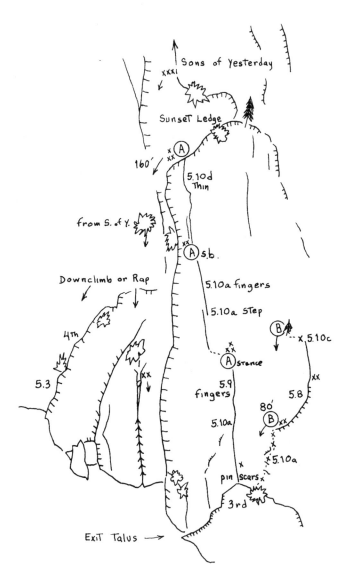

SERENITY CRACK AREA

Travel a short distance east of the Ahwahnee Hotel along the horse trail. At the first creekbed, head up left along the wall for a couple hundred feet. The higher of two emerging ledge systems leads to a perch at the start of this striking crack.

A **Serenity Crack 5.10d** ★★★ Pro from ¼ to 2 inches, especially ⅜ to 1½ inch pieces. This climb offers beautifully continuous finger jamming over three pitches. Elegant and civilized. The first pitch is badly pin-scarred.

B **Maxine's Wall 5.10c** ★ Pro to 2 inches (only QDs needed for the first pitch). Most parties do only one pitch—mostly friction and edging.

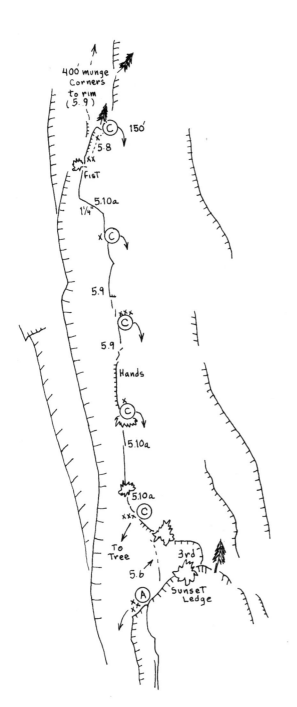

C Sons of Yesterday 5.10a
★★★ Pro to 3½ inches, especially ¾ to 2 inch pieces. Offers an enjoyable altitude gain. Stance belays.

ROYAL ARCHES

1 **Bishop's Terrace**
2 **Serenity Crack**
3 **Royal Arches Route**

ROYAL ARCHES

4 Arches Terrace Area

ROYAL ARCHES

Hike east from the Ahwahnee Hotel on the horse trail. About 100 feet after crossing a small creek, head up the hill to the first pitch chimney.

DESCENT Scramble down North Dome Gully which starts near the top of Washington Column. From the Column, travel east to the forested gully; stay above the death slabs. This descent is the scene of frequent accidents: take care. Don't descend too early; if in doubt and contemplating rappels, keep traversing. If unfamiliar with the descent, don't try it at night.

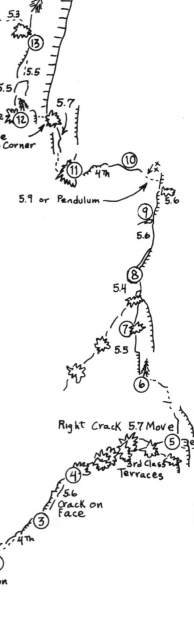

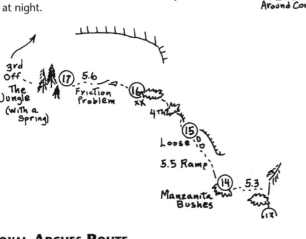

ROYAL ARCHES ROUTE

5.7 A1 or 5.9 ★★ Pro to 2½ inches. This is the most popular lengthy route of its difficulty in the valley. Although a few unpleasant sections are encountered, the climbing is generally enjoyable with an adventuresome setting.

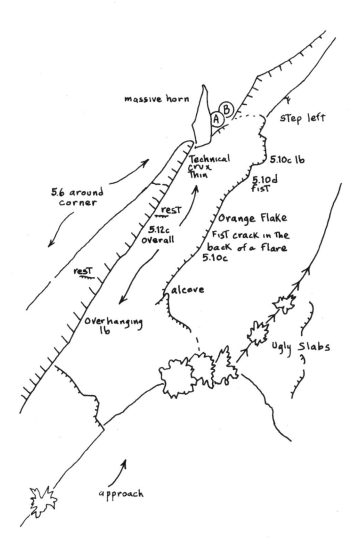

massive horn

A B

sTep left

Technical crux Thin

5.10c lb

5.10d FisT

5.6 around corner

resT

5.12c overall

Orange Flake

FisT crack in The back of a flare 5.10c

resT

alcove

Overhanging lb

Ugly Slabs

approach

ROYAL ARCHES—ARCHES TERRACE AREA

Walk several hundred yards east along the horse trail from the Ahwahnee Hotel before striking steeply up the hill.

A **Hangdog Flyer 5.12c** ★★ Pro: small to 2 inches, especially ¾ to 1½ inch pieces. Exhausting. Up high, a long reach is helpful.

B **10.96 5.10d** ★★ Pro: ¾ to 3½ inch, especially 2½ to 3 inch pieces. A punishing route on beautiful rock.

NORTH DOME

The routes on North Dome are often approached by doing the Royal Arches Route, see page *82. Otherwise, walk in from the Tioga Road on the North Dome Trail(about 4.5 miles to summit) and skirt down the west side of the Dome, or slog up North Dome Gully, described on page 82.

DESCENT   Walk off the west side of the dome and hike down North Dome Gully, as described on page 82.

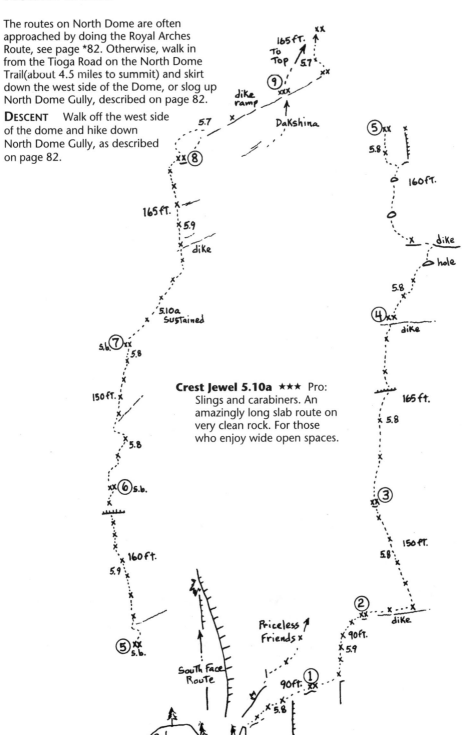

165 ft.
To Top
57
9
Dakshina
dike ramp
5.7

5
5.8
160 ft.
dike
hole
5.8
4
dike
165 ft.
5.8

8
165 ft.
5.9
dike
5.10a
Sustained
5.b. 7
5.8
150 ft.
5.8
xx 6 5.b.
160 ft.
5.9
5 5.b.

Crest Jewel 5.10a ★★★ Pro: Slings and carabiners. An amazingly long slab route on very clean rock. For those who enjoy wide open spaces.

3
150 ft.
5.8
2
dike
Priceless Friends
90 ft.
5.9
South Face Route
90 ft. 1
5.8
3rd

NORTH DOME
Crest Jewell

⑤

A1

5.11   160'

x̶x̶   A2

165' To   x   Skull
Dinner   ④   Queen
     x

5.11

A1

Kor Roof

5.6

xx③xx Dinner Ledge
bivy   5.6

   5.8

②
   xx

5.10a

5.11b or A1
1b

5.10a   ①xx

Rotten
Slabs
& Cracks   5.6 Ramp

5.8   The Prow

4Th Class

Washington Column

From the Ahwahnee Hotel or North Pines Campground, take the trail toward Indian Caves. Before the caves are reached, however, head up north (near a point where the bike path and the horse trail almost touch), and follow the drainage that comes down from the left side of the Column. A climber's trail skirts the base of the cliff all the way east to the bottom of North Dome Gully.

Descent Routes that end atop Washington Column necessitate a familiarity with North Dome Gully, the easiest access to and from the rim. The descent down North Dome Gully is the scene of frequent accidents. The trail from the top of the column traverses east all the way to the forested gully, and completely above the death slabs. Don't descend too early; if in doubt, and contemplating a rappel, keep traversing. If unfamiliar with the descent, don't attempt it at night.

Washington Column— South Face

V 5.9 A2 ★★ Hardware—
Nuts to 3 inches, including many ⅛ to 1½ inch pieces. The most popular grade V in the valley.

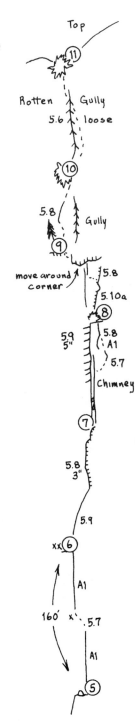

Top

⑪

Rotten   Gully
5.6   loose

⑩

5.8   Gully

⑨

move around   5.8
corner
     5.10a

⑧

5.9   5.8
5"   A1
     5.7

Chimney

⑦

5.8
3"

5.9

xx⑥

A1

160' x .5.7

A1

⑤

WASHINGTON COLUMN—EAST FACE

NPS photo

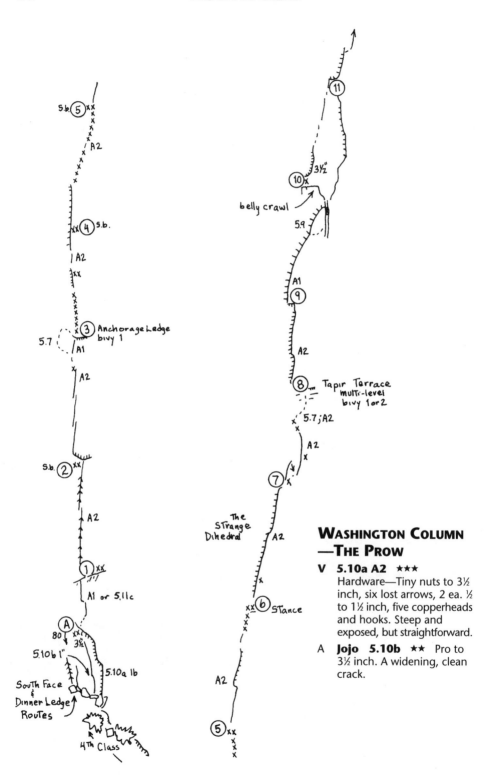

5.b. ⑤ xx
x
x
A2
x
x
x
x

xx ④ 5.b.
x
| A2
x xx
x
x x x x x
x x
③ Anchorage Ledge
5.7 (x bivy 1
| A1
x
| A2
|
|

S.b. ② xx
x
x
| A2
x
x
x
x
① xx
/
A1 or 5.11c
Ⓐ xx
80 3¼
5.10b 1"
5.10a 1b
South Face
&
Dinner Ledge
Routes
4th Class

↑
⑪
3½"
⑩ x
belly crawl
5.9
A1
⑨
A2
⑧ Tapir Terrace
multi-level
bivy 1 or 2
x 5.7; A2
A2
x
⑦ x
The
Strange
Dihedral A2
x
xx ⑥ Stance
x
x
A2
⑤ xx
x
x
x

Washington Column
—The Prow

V 5.10a A2 ★★★
Hardware—Tiny nuts to 3½
inch, six lost arrows, 2 ea. ½
to 1½ inch, five copperheads
and hooks. Steep and
exposed, but straightforward.

A **Jojo 5.10b** ★★ Pro to
3½ inch. A widening, clean
crack.

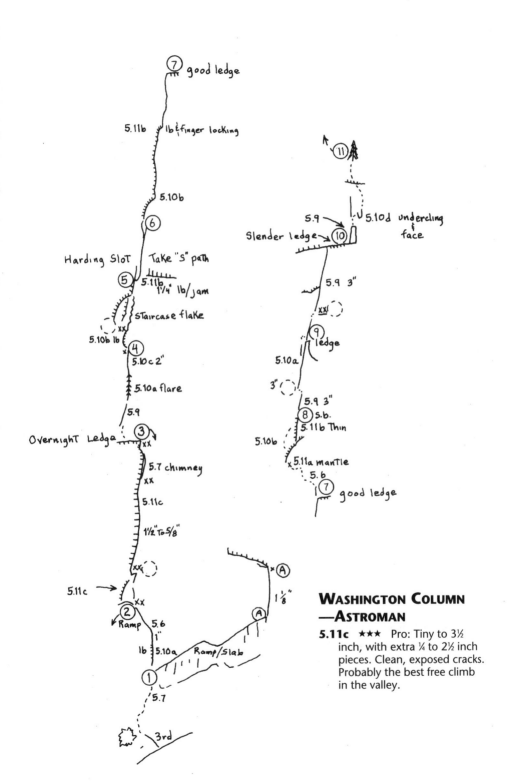

WASHINGTON COLUMN —ASTROMAN

5.11c ★★★ Pro: Tiny to 3½ inch, with extra ¼ to 2½ inch pieces. Clean, exposed cracks. Probably the best free climb in the valley.

HALF DOME—NORTHWEST FACE

NPS photo

HALF DOME—NORTHWEST FACE

Hike up from Happy Isles to the eastern shoulder of Half Dome (about 7.5 miles). From the broad wooded ridge before the cables and sandy switchbacks, drop down and around to the base of the northwest face via a climber's trail. A quicker, more direct, yet very devious approach can be made from the vicinity of Mirror Lake. In general, this begins somewhat upstream from Mirror Lake, trending up and right, with the final section ascending beneath Tis-sa-ack, the lighter colored rock on the right side of the face.

A **Final Exam 5.10d** ★★★   Pro: 2 to 3½ inches, expecially 2½ to 3 inch pieces. The first pitch features incredible jamming in a perfect corner. Renovation of the rap anchor may be appropriate. The second pitch generally is avoided.

NORTHWEST FACE—REGULAR ROUTE

VI 5.9 A2 or 5.12 ★★★   Pro: two to three nuts of each size to 3 inches, Friends. Climbing on the lower section is somewhat devious. After the traverse to the right, at about the eleventh pitch, the cracks are better defined and the climbing more straightforward. This route sees much traffic by both aspiring big-wall climbers and one-day speed ascent teams. Other climbers and loose rock warrant consideration and respect while on the face.

HALF DOME—NORTHWEST FACE REGULAR ROUTE

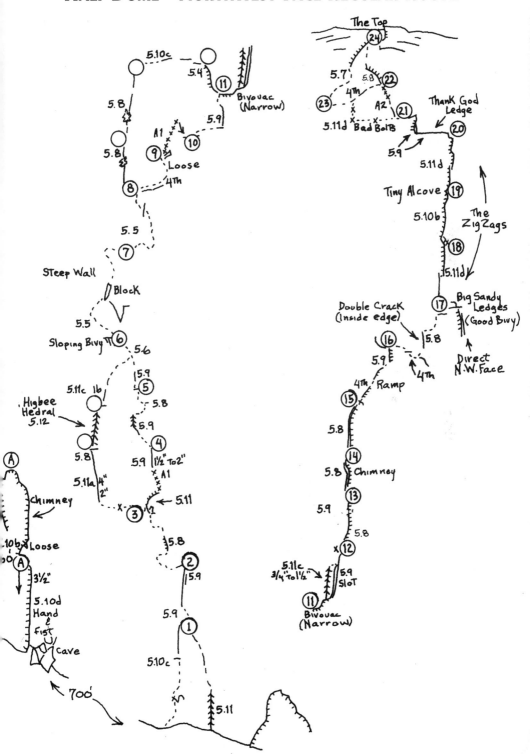

Snake
Dike

HALF DOME—SOUTHWEST FACE

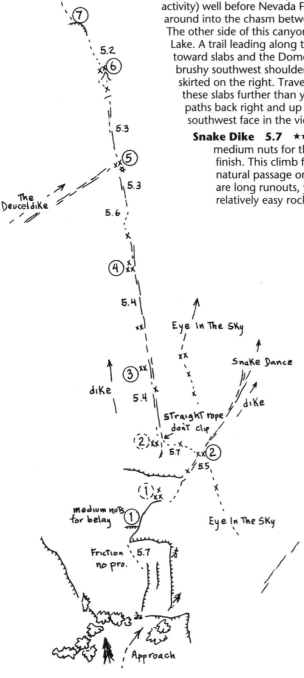

1,000 ft. Class2 friction To Summit ⑧

5.2

⑦

5.2
xx ⑥
x

5.3

xx ⑤
❄

The Deuceldike

5.3

5.6

x

④ x
xx

5.4

xx

③ xx

dike

5.4

Eye In The Sky

xx

Snake Dance

dike

STraight rope
dont clip

② xx   x
5.7   xx ②

x 5.5

① x
xx

medium nuts
for belay ①

Eye In The Sky

Friction 5.7
no pro.

Approach

HALF DOME—SOUTHWEST FACE

Hike up from Happy Isles toward Little Yosemite. Once the trail levels out above Nevada Falls, walk up a short hillside and work to the north and west, to Lost Lake. Lost Lake may also be reached from between Mount Broderick and Liberty Cap. In this case, work up talus slopes under the northwest corner of Liberty Cap (site of recent rockfall activity) well before Nevada Falls is reached, and contour around into the chasm between the two formations. The other side of this canyon opens out directly at Lost Lake. A trail leading along the lake's left side heads up toward slabs and the Dome. Slabs that lie under the brushy southwest shoulder of Half Dome are best skirted on the right. Traverse left on ledges above these slabs further than you think and follow rough paths back right and up to the base of the southwest face in the vicinity of the Snake Dike.

Snake Dike 5.7 ★★★ Pro: A few small to medium nuts for the belays at the start and finish. This climb follows a phenomenal natural passage on a grand monolith. There are long runouts, yet the climbing is on relatively easy rock.

The Grack

The Cow

GLACIER POINT APRON—EAST SIDE

The eastern portion of the Glacier Point Apron was decimated by a huge, spontaneous rock fall in the summer of 1996. Although the real impact area was east or left of the Cow and the Grack, these climbs lie on the fringe of a bona fide death zone. Future catastrophic events of this nature can not be predicted, therefore the utmost discretion must be used when considering these climbs. Happy Isles and the old approach are wiped out so the only reasonable approach would be from the west, closer to Curry Village.

GLACIER POINT APRON—EAST

A **The Cow—Left 5.8** ★ Pro: A few pieces for the second pitch. Low angle but smooth and runout.

B **The Cow—Center 5.5** ★ Pro to 2½ inch.

C **The Grack—Center 5.6** ★★★ Pro to 2 inch. Three pitches on a low-angle slab via a snaking crack. Nut belays with small stances. The crack stops just short of the top.

D **The Grack—Marginal 5.9** ★★★ Pro: A few pieces, tiny to 1¼ inch. A sea of friction.

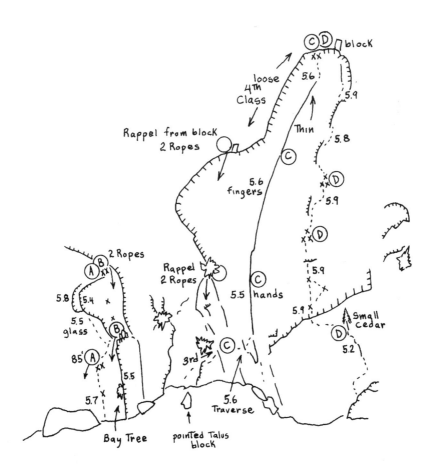

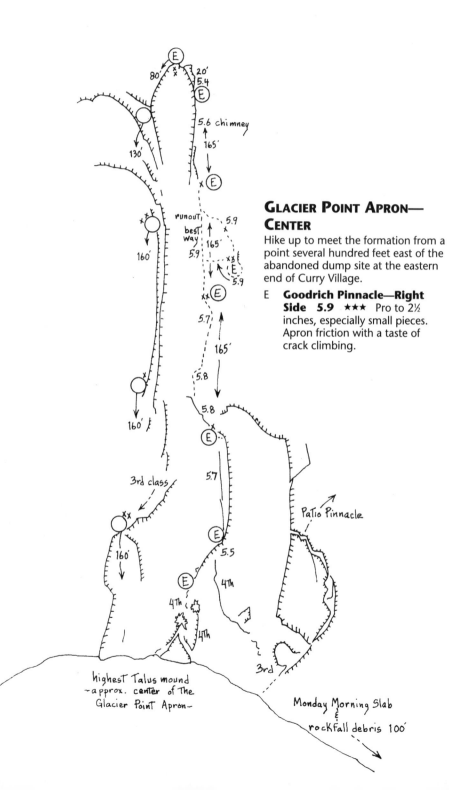

GLACIER POINT APRON—CENTER

Hike up to meet the formation from a point several hundred feet east of the abandoned dump site at the eastern end of Curry Village.

E   **Goodrich Pinnacle—Right Side 5.9** ★★★ Pro to 2½ inches, especially small pieces. Apron friction with a taste of crack climbing.

Dave Page on Snake Dike

Walter J. Flint

CHAPEL WALL

A horse trail runs along the base of the cliff. Begin from the chapel and walk southwest or down-valley along the trail for several hundred feet. At a level spot leading to the cliff, Heathenistic Pursuit can be seen as a huge, left-facing corner 100 feet away.

A surge of recent development has taken place on this cliff. Many of the newer routes are bolt-protected, vertical faces that exhibit edging cranks and side pulls.

A **Colors 5.12b** ★★ Pro: QDs.

B **New Wave 5.11d** ★★ Pro: QDs.

C **Heathenistic Pursuit 5.10b** ★★ Pro to 2½ inches.

D **Gold Dust 5.10d** ★★ Pro to 2½ inches, plus additional small pieces.

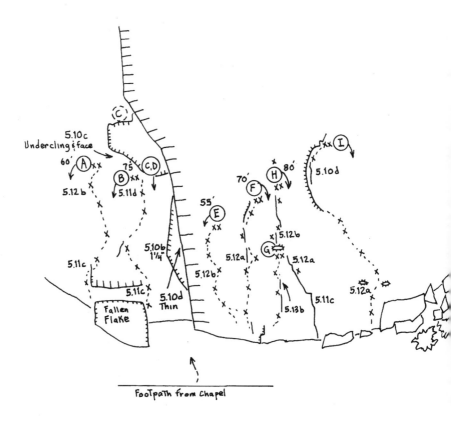

Footpath from Chapel

E **Berlin Wall 5.12b** ★ Pro: QDs.

F **Drive By Shooting 5.12a** ★★★ Pro: QDs, a #2 Friend.

G **Cripps 5.13b** ★ Pro: QDs, a few pieces.

H **Double Dragon 5.12b** ★★ Pro: QDs, a few wires and TCUs.

I **House of Pain 5.12a** ★★ Pro: QDs, a few pieces.

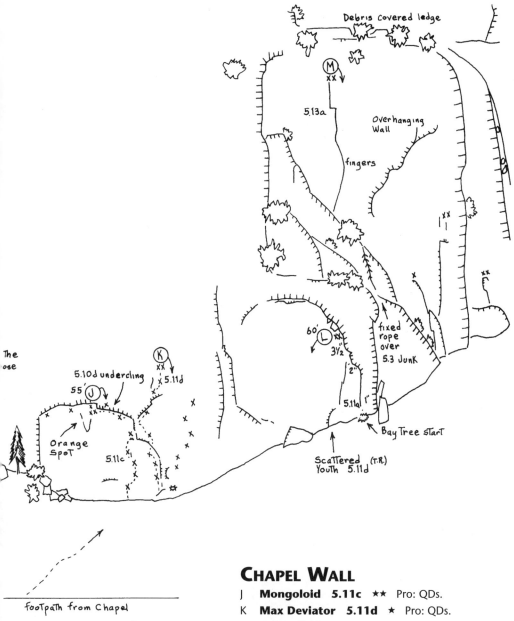

Debris covered ledge

M
xx ↓

5.13a

Overhanging Wall

fingers

60'
L
xx
3½"

fixed rope over 5.3 Junk

2"

5.11a 1"

Bay Tree start

The ose

K
xx
x 5.11d

5.10d undercling

55' J
xx
xx x

Orange Spot

5.11c

Scattered (T.R.)
Youth 5.11d

footpath from Chapel

CHAPEL WALL

J **Mongoloid 5.11c** ★★ Pro: QDs.

K **Max Deviator 5.11d** ★ Pro: QDs.

L **Controlled Burn 5.11a** ★★ Pro: ¼ to 3½ inches. A deteriorating bay tree accesses this short but pumping crack.

M **Cosmic Debris 5.13b** ★★★ Pro: ⅜ to 1½ inch, especially ¾ inch pieces. Sustained overhanging finger locking, with one hand jam. A half-rope length long.

Mary Hinson (Littel) on top of the Lost Arrow Spire
Walter J. Flint

Chouinard-Herbert

Steck-Salathé   West Face

SENTINEL ROCK

The routes on the north and west faces of Sentinel Rock are approached by third-class ledges that traverse up and right across the lower, broken area of the formation. First, hike up the Four-Mile Trail for about a mile to the stream that comes down from the east side of the rock. Leave the trail, and hike up the stream bed several hundred feet, then move over to the prominent ramp that starts the long scramble up and right. This leads to the base of the Flying Buttress, an 800-foot pillar that sits at the right side of the flat, north face, and is the start of the Flying Buttress Direct and the Steck Salathé. The routes on the west face are around the corner. The routes on the north face require further scrambling up and left on ledges. Allow two hours approach time from Camp 4.

DESCENT From the summit, work south to the notch behind Sentinel Rock via manzanita tunnels that skirt small outcrops. From the notch, scramble down the loose, Class 2 gully that leads east to a stream. Further down, descend improbable terrain in the middle of a scruffy buttress that separates two chasms. Eventually, Four-Mile Trail is reached.

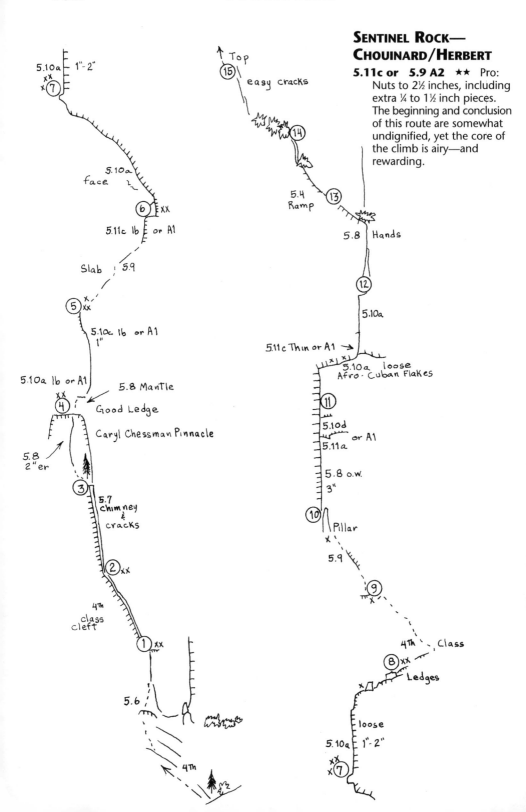

SENTINEL ROCK— CHOUINARD/HERBERT

5.11c or 5.9 A2 ★★ Pro: Nuts to 2½ inches, including extra ¼ to 1½ inch pieces. The beginning and conclusion of this route are somewhat undignified, yet the core of the climb is airy—and rewarding.

5.10a 1"- 2"
x x
x (7)

5.10a
face

(6) XX
5.11c lb or A1

Slab   5.9

(5) x
xx

5.10c lb or A1
1"

5.10a lb or A1
XX
(4)   5.8 Mantle
Good Ledge

Caryl Chessman Pinnacle

5.8
2"er

(3)   5.7
chimney
&
cracks

(2) xx

4th
class
cleft

(1) xx

5.6

4th

↑ Top
(15)   easy cracks

(14)

5.4
Ramp   (13)

5.8   Hands

(12)

5.10a

5.11c Thin or A1 →
x x
5.10a   loose
Afro- Cuban Flakes

(11)

5.10d
or A1
5.11a

5.8 o.w.
3"

(10)   Pillar
x

5.9

(9)
x

4th   Class

(8) xx
Ledges
x

loose

5.10a 1"- 2"
xx
x (7)

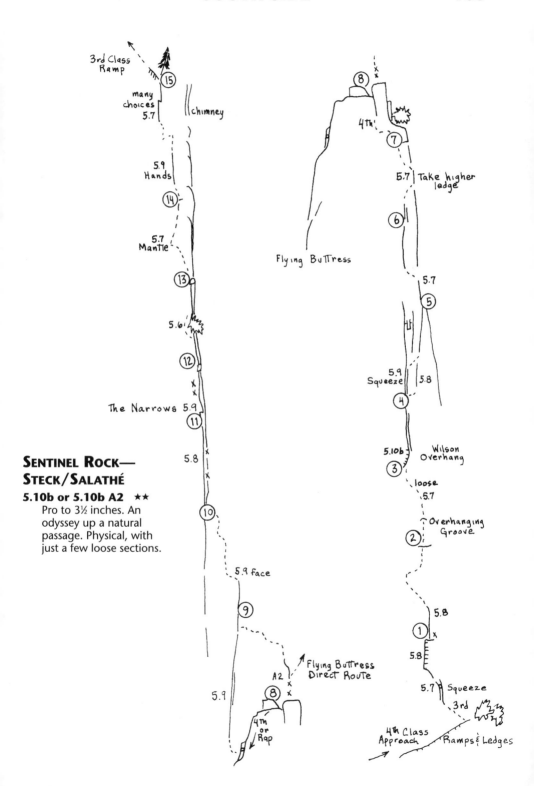

3rd Class Ramp

⑮ many choices 5.7 | chimney

5.9 Hands

⑭

5.7 Mantle

⑬

5.6

⑫

The Narrows 5.9 ⑪

5.8

**SENTINEL ROCK—
STECK/SALATHÉ**

5.10b or 5.10b A2 ★★

Pro to 3½ inches. An odyssey up a natural passage. Physical, with just a few loose sections.

⑩

5.9 face

⑨

A2 | Flying Buttress Direct Route

5.9

⑧ 4th or Rap

⑧

4th

⑦ 5.7 | Take higher ledge

⑥

Flying Buttress

5.7 ⑤

5.9 Squeeze | 5.8

④

5.10b Wilson Overhang

③

loose 5.7

Overhanging Groove

②

5.8

① 5.8

5.7 | Squeeze

3rd

4th Class Approach | Ramps & Ledges

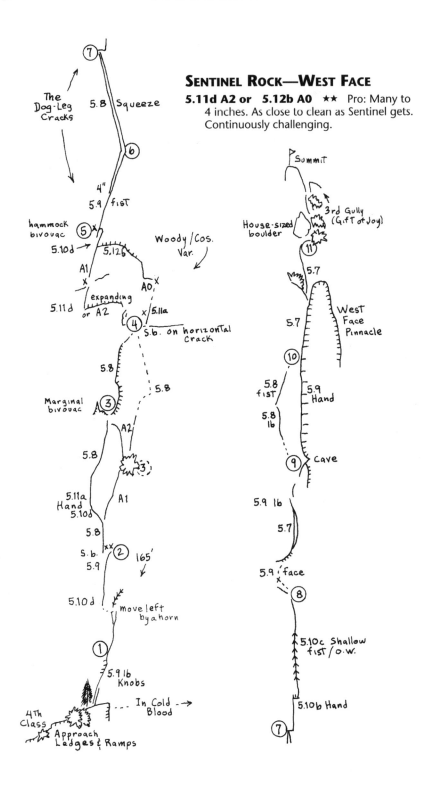

SENTINEL ROCK—WEST FACE

5.11d A2 or 5.12b A0 ★★ Pro: Many to
4 inches. As close to clean as Sentinel gets.
Continuously challenging.

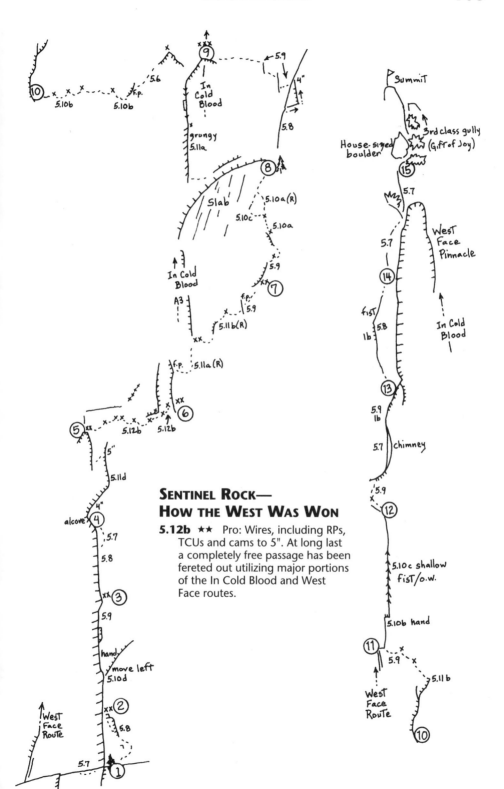

SENTINEL ROCK—
HOW THE WEST WAS WON

5.12b ★★ Pro: Wires, including RPs, TCUs and cams to 5". At long last a completely free passage has been fereted out utilizing major portions of the In Cold Blood and West Face routes.

HIGHER CATHEDRAL ROCK—EAST FACE

NPS photo

1 **Higher Cathedral Spire**   4 **Mary's Tears**
2 **Lower Cathedral Spire**   5 **Northeast Buttress**
3 **Braille Book**   6 **Crucifix**

HIGHER CATHEDRAL ROCK

The routes on Higher Cathedral are approached via the climber's trail up the Spires Gully. This leads ultimately to the notch between Higher Cathedral Rock and the wall that is up and behind Cathedral Spires. Start hiking at a road turnout 1.4 miles east of the Highway 41/Highway 140 junction at Bridalveil Falls. The trial heads directly back into the woods and up.

DESCENT   From the summit of Higher Cathedral Rock, walk south and around to the upper part of the Spires Gully.

THE BRAILLE BOOK

5.8 ★★★   Pro to 3 inches. Steep crack climbing amid abundant knobs rewards a trudge approach.

Descend To Spires Gully

⑤

5.4
Knob Mania

5.7
④

5.8
④

5.10c Var.
5.8 STem
③
chimney/flare

5.7

5.6

②

5.8 fist

160'

5.7

①

5.7

f p

The Book of Job

The Dictionary (big & way ugly)

Spires Gully

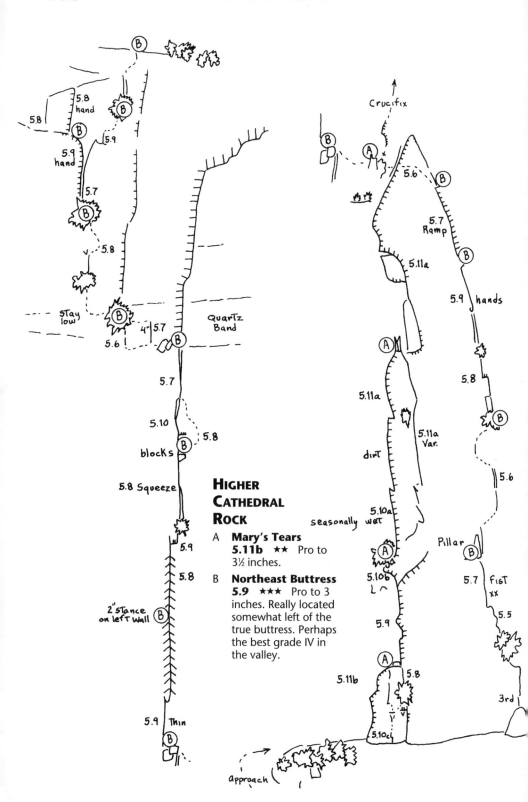

B

5.8
hand

5.8

B

5.9

B

5.9
hand

5.7

B

5.8

v

STay
low

B

4" 5.7

5.6 !

B

Quartz
Band

Crucifix

B

A

5.6

B

5.7
Ramp

B

5.11a

5.9   hands

A

5.8

B

5.11a

5.11a
Var.

5.6

dirt

5.7

5.10

blocks

B

5.8

5.8 Squeeze

5.9

5.8

2" stance
on lefT wall

B

5.9 | Thin

B

seasonally wet

5.10a

HIGHER CATHEDRAL ROCK

A   **Mary's Tears**
5.11b ★★   Pro to
3½ inches.

B   **Northeast Buttress**
5.9 ★★★   Pro to 3
inches. Really located
somewhat left of the
true buttress. Perhaps
the best grade IV in
the valley.

A

5.10b
L

5.9

A

5.11b

5.8

5.10c

Pillar

B

5.7   FIST
xx

5.5

3rd

approach

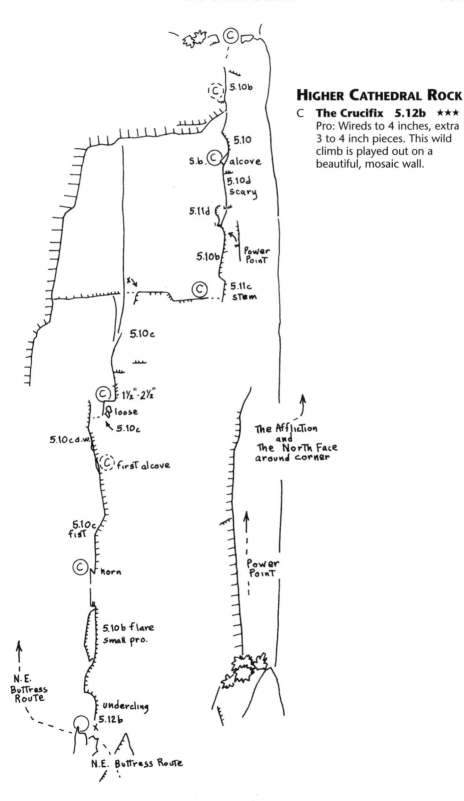

HIGHER CATHEDRAL ROCK

C **The Crucifix 5.12b** ★★★
Pro: Wireds to 4 inches, extra 3 to 4 inch pieces. This wild climb is played out on a beautiful, mosaic wall.

5.10b

5.10

S.b. alcove

5.10d scary

5.11d

5.10b — Power Point

5.11c stem

5.10c

1½"-2½"

loose

5.10c

5.10c o.w.

first alcove

5.10c fist

horn

The Affliction and The North Face around corner

Power Point

5.10b flare small pro.

N.E. Buttress Route

undercling
5.12b

N.E. Buttress Route

THE CATHEDRAL ROCKS

NPS photo

1 **Braille Book**
2 **Northeast Buttress**
3 **East Buttress**
4 **Central Pillar of Frenzy**
5 **Stoner's Highway**
6 **Direct North Buttress**

MIDDLE CATHEDRAL ROCK

The East Buttress of Middle Cathedral Rock is hiked to from a turnout 1.3 miles from the Highway 41/Highway 140 junction at Bridalveil Falls. For Central Pillar, Stoner's Highway and Direct North Buttress, park in the same vicinity and hike back west to the rock via the horse trail that parallels the road in the woods to the south.

DESCENT   While most of the routes of the northeast face do not lead to the summit, all that do eventually cross the Kat Walk, a fault line/ledge system that traverses the rock from the top of the DNB, east to the East Buttress and on into the Cathedral Chimney, the great chasm that lies between Middle and Higher Cathedral Rocks. The goal of climbers ascending the East Buttress and routes that climb up in that vicinity is to scramble up from the top of the technical climbing to the Kat Walk, which here is an area of sloping meadows and heavy brush. Work left toward the Cathedral Chimney, where some minor downclimbing leads to talus and the valley floor. A descent of the upper part of the Cathedral Chimney requires rappels, and the goal of the descending climber is to work left toward the chimney below this point.

Other routes on the northeast face of Middle (like Stoner's Highway) are best rappelled from their high points, but if the choice is to continue, they most often lead to the Powell-Reed Ledges, a sweeping and broad system that leads up and left into the U-shaped Bowl. With some careful route-finding, a moderate fifth-class scramble can be made up and out the left side of this feature to the Kat Walk. The Direct North Buttress and North Buttress lead to a spot behind Thirsty Spire, a lone pinnacle at the west end of the Kat Walk. Either walk left along the ledge system to the Cathedral Chimney or continue on easy fifth class for 300 feet to brushy slopes that lead to the summit.

From the summit of Middle Cathedral, there are several choices. One can walk down to the notch between Middle and Higher, scramble up to the top of Higher, and then walk south to the top of the Spires Gully and the trail that leads down from there. Alternatively, steep slabs on the northeast side of the rock can be descended (with possible rappels) to the Kat Walk, where a scramble south leads to the Cathedral Chimney below the difficulties. Finally, it is possible to bushwhack down the west side of Middle for a descent down the Gunsight, the notch between Middle and Lower Rocks. From the notch between Middle and Lower Rocks, walk down brush-covered slabs that lead west for about 400 feet, or until very steep slabs are encountered. Traverse left into a thick brushfield, then head straight down toward Bridalveil Creek. When about 200 feet above the water, contour north and head uphill for the top of the Gunsight. Scrambling and short rappels lead to talus and the valley floor.

Middle Cathedral Rock— East Buttress

5.9 A1 or 5.10c ★★★ Pro to 2½ inches. Very popular.

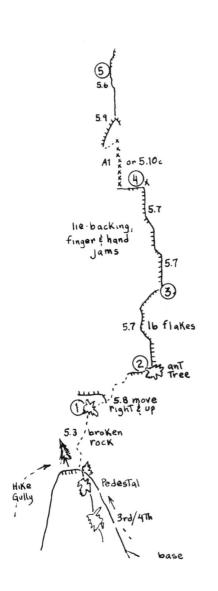

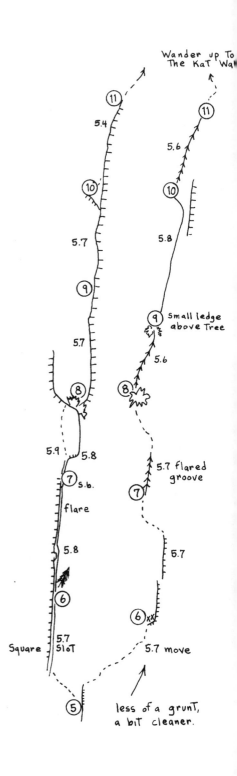

Wander up To The KaT Wa[l]

5.4

5.6

5.7

5.8

5.7

5.6

small ledge above Tree

5.7

5.7 flared groove

5.7

5.9   5.8

7 5.6.

flare

5.8

5.7 Slot

Square

5.7 move

less of a grunT, a biT cleaner.

5 5.6

5.9

A1 or 5.10c

5.7

lie·backing, finger & hand jams

5.7

5.7 lb flakes

anT Tree

5.8 move righT & up

5.3 broken rock

Hike Gully

Pedestal

3rd/4Th

base

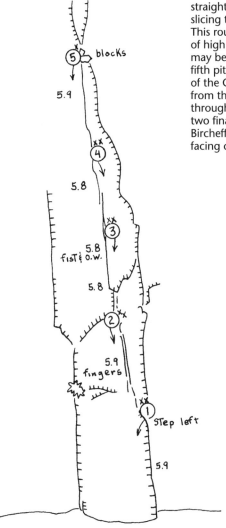

blocks

5.9

5.8

5.8
fist & o.w.

5.8

5.9
fingers

step left

5.9

MIDDLE CATHEDRAL ROCK— CENTRAL PILLAR OF FRENZY

5.9 (first five pitches only) ★★★ Pro: ⅜ to 3½ inch, especially ½ to 2 inch pieces. A straightforward and aesthetic crack system slicing the face of Middle Cathedral Rock. This route draws a crowd. During periods of high traffic, an alternate rappel route may be used to avoid congestion. From the fifth pitch rappel to bolt stations that lie left of the Central Pillar Route (as one looks up from the ground). The initial rappels pass through the Grand Wazoo Route and the two final rappels are made from the Bircheff/Williams, the prominent left-facing corner. Two ropes are still necessary.

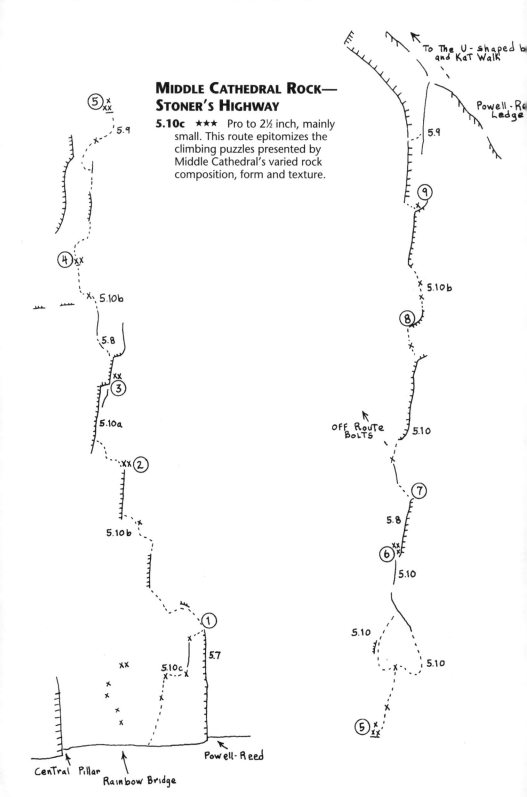

MIDDLE CATHEDRAL ROCK—STONER'S HIGHWAY

5.10c ★★★ Pro to 2½ inch, mainly small. This route epitomizes the climbing puzzles presented by Middle Cathedral's varied rock composition, form and texture.

MIDDLE CATHEDRAL ROCK—
DIRECT NORTH BUTTRESS

(AKA DNB) 5.10b ★★★ Pro to 3 inches, including extra ⅛ to 1 inch pieces. Though not immaculate, still one of the cleanest and longest climbs on Middle Cathedral Rock.

13

5.8 1b

5.9 | 2"

12 alcove s.b.

5.9

11

5.7 | 165'

5.9

5 Powell·Reed Ledges

5.9 5.7

10

5.9 5.7

4 5.8 o.w. flare

5.9

9

3

5.10b

2 5.7 1b

5.7 flakes 5.8

8

1 5.8

5.7

Chimney

7

100' To The Kat Walk

4Th

17 Thirsty Spire

5.8 | Jam

16

5.7 Jam

15

5.6 Slot

The Turret

14

4Th

13

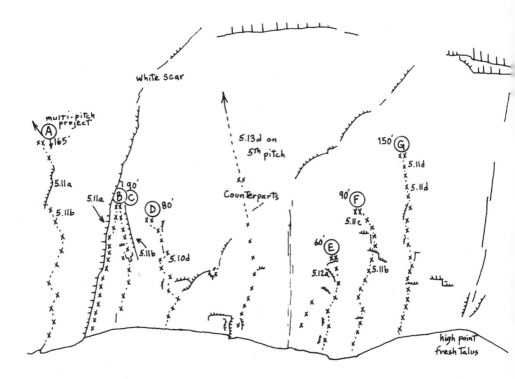

Lower Cathedral Rock-Mecca (North Face base routes)

Approach   Traveling 0.3 mile toward the valley from the junction of the Valley loop and Hwy. 41(Bridalveil Falls Parking Lot), park in the long turnout which parallels the straight section of road. Skirt the split rail fence and hike the trail as it climbs slightly, moving up-valley. Upon reaching open talus, with a huge dead tree embedded in the rockfall, work up to the base of the cliff. Rockfall potential makes this area a little spooky, but the views of El Capitan are outstanding. A cool area in the heat. Please stay current with possible Peregrine Falcon closures.

A   **The Pilgrimage 5.11b** ★★   (1st pitch only shown) Pro. to 2½ inches.

B   **Scrubby Corner 5.11a** ★★   Pro: QDs. A clip and climb classic with the crux forcing a move out right at the top.

C   **Meccaphobia 5.11b** ★★   Pro: QDs. Slightly sporty, yet the bouldering-type crux, up high, is well protected.

D   **Peasant 5.10d** ★   Pro. QDs.

E   **Mechanical Advantage 5.12a** ★★   Pro. QDs.

F   **King and I 5.11c** ★★

G   **King for a Day 5.11d** ★★

H **Filthy Savage 5.10b** ★ Pro to 3 inches. Wires and TCUs make the first two bolts unnecessary. Twenty feet above the bolt anchor is a 5.10d move and a bail-out anchor at the roof.

I **Rock Monkey Rebellion 5.11a** ★ Pro. QDs. Thin crux moves at the small white arch.

J **Eye of the Hurricane 5.11a** ★★ Pro: QDs.

K **Gorilla Gardens 5.10d** ★ Pro to 3 inches. From skinny branches abstract jamming lies above.

L **Empire 5.13a** ★★ Pro: QDs.

M **Giblet 5.10c** ★ Pro: QDs. Seven bolts, 1 fixed pin. However, with a selection to 2 inches and a few runners the second bolt is the only one necessary.

N **Tidbit 5.10d** ★ Pro: Wires and several TCUs; include one 3½" piece for the top. The hard-core excperience is Giblet and Tidbit done in one pitch.

O **Velvet Elvis 5.12a** ★ Pro: QDs. Formerly rated 5.11b, a key hold has broken. A new and harder variation with additional bolts (bolt count uncertain) has now been established.

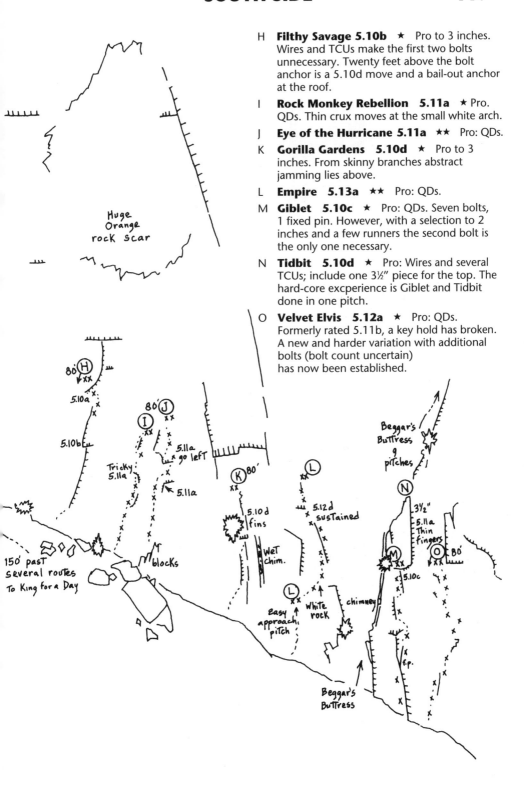

Mecca Area

LOWER CATHEDRAL ROCK—NORTH FACE

Walter J. Flint

LOWER CATHEDRAL ROCK

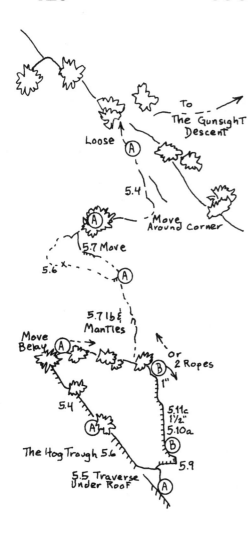

LOWER CATHEDRAL ROCK

These routes are approached from the long parking turnout below and up-valley from Bridalveil Falls. Scramble up talus and third class rock to the routes, marked by the clean, gray corner that is Overhang Overpass.

DESCENT   These routes end on the west slopes of Lower Cathedral Rock. From here, contour along to meet the Gunsight, the notch between Middle and Lower Cathedral Rocks. A short rappel or two may be necessary in this section.

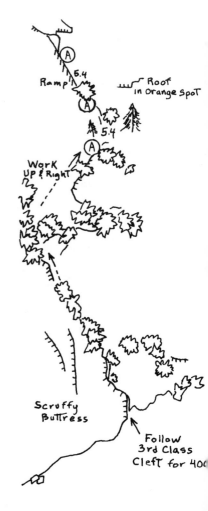

A   **Overhang Bypass 5.7** ★★   Pro to 2½ inches. The route is taxed by a fairly involved approach and descent. The rock is compact and cleanly fractured, with the "hog trough" being particularly clean and exposed. However, some loose rock is also found on this route.

B   **Overhang Overpass 5.11c** ★★★   Pro to 2½ inches, including extra ½ to 1¾ inch pieces. A burdensome approach and descent are warranted by this striking corner.

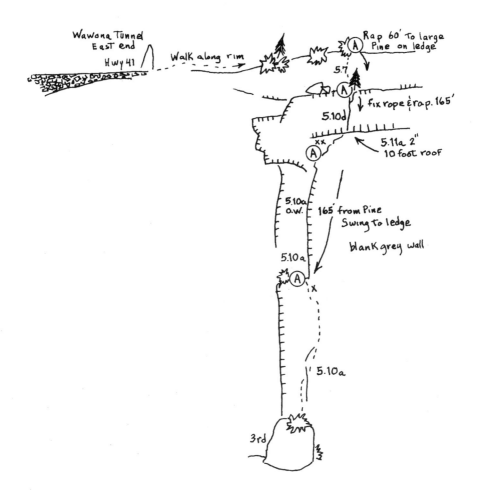

DISCOVERY VIEW

Overdrive is located on the cliff below the Wawona Tunnel, near Discovery View, commonly but not accurately referred to as Inspiration Point. Although it is possible to approach from below, it is much more convenient to forego the first pitch, and come in from above. Do this via a short walk and a couple of rappels.

A **Overdrive 5.11a** ★ Pro to 3½ inches (also a 'fixed' rappel rope). Semi-obscure, yet close to the road. Features an exhilarating roof experience.

PULPIT ROCK

APPROACH   Park in the lot at the Highway 140/Highway 120 junction. The river crossing is only possible during periods of low water. Beware poison oak!

B   **The Sermon 5.10b** ★★
Pro to 3 1/2 inches. This is the prominent crack line on the formation. It can be pumping in the middle and a bit burly at the top.

C   **Magilla Gorilla 5.11b** ★★
Pro: QDs , TCU optional

D   **Gorilla Cookies 5.10d** ★
Pro QDs , TCU. optional (chainlink bolt hangers).

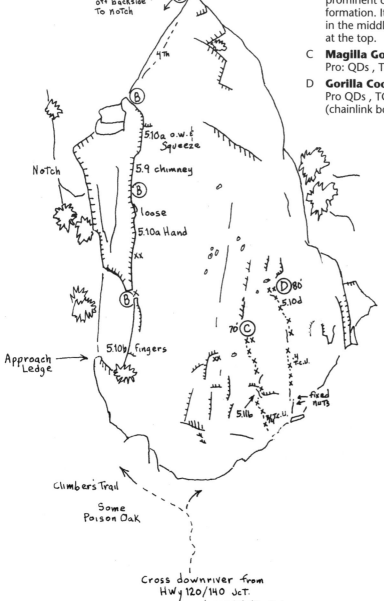

Two 80' Raps off backside To Notch

4th

5.10a o.w. & Squeeze

Notch

5.9 chimney

loose

5.10a Hand

xx

5.10b fingers

Approach Ledge

80

5.10d

70

xx

4 T.c.u.

fixed nuts

5.11b

4 T.c.u.

Climber's Trail

Some Poison Oak

Cross downriver from Hwy 120/140 Jct.
Low Water Only

WAWONA TUNNEL, WEST END—
THE BLOWHOLE

APPROACH Park at the west end of the Wawona Tunnel. Walk back into the tunnel then enter the smaller side-vent tunnel(the Blowhole), which once again leads to the outside world. A two bolt anchor is found just beyond the grate, a site that allows packs or other personal gear to remain in sight while on the climbs. This is a cool area in the summer and may even provide ice climbing potential in winter. The climbing is on water polished rock, yet features fingertip in-cuts and small scale, route finding problems. Almost entirely bolt protected, a token TCU and a few wired nuts may prove helpful for some.

A **Thar She Blows 5.11a** ★★
B **Honk If You're Horny 5.10c** ★★
C **Wind Tunnel 5.10b** ★
D **The Fledgling 5.10a** ★
E **Fire In The Hole 5.10b** ★
F **Variation 5.10a** ★★

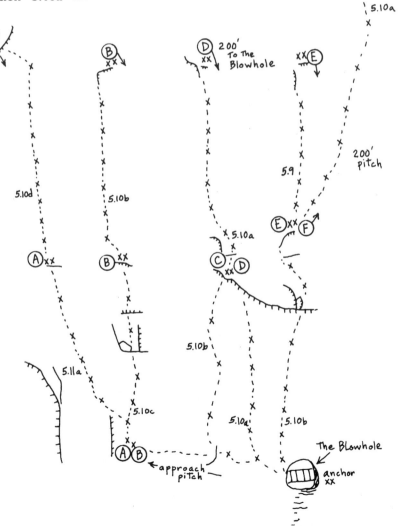

CREAM AREA

These climbs are located on a faceted buttress below Highway 41. Park a half mile past the west end of the Wawona Tunnel, just before the long, stone wall.

A　**Cream　5.11a**　★★　Pro: 2 to 6 inches, including extra 4 to 6 inch pieces. A bizarre approach, yet a remarkable crack. A must for the offwidth aficionado. The crux is a slightly overhanging section perhaps 60 feet up, where the knee has to come out for a move. Physical but fairly secure above.

B　**Jam Session　5.10b**　★　Pro: 2 to 5 inches. The junior version of Cream.

C　**Energy Crisis　5.11d**　★★★　Pro to 2 inches, including extra #1½ and especially #2 Friends. Basically, this climb is 85 feet of off-hand jamming. The technical crux is a slightly thinner, bulging section at the halfway point, but endurance over the distance is the name of the game.

Across the Valley at New Diversions
Walter J. Flint

CREAM AREA

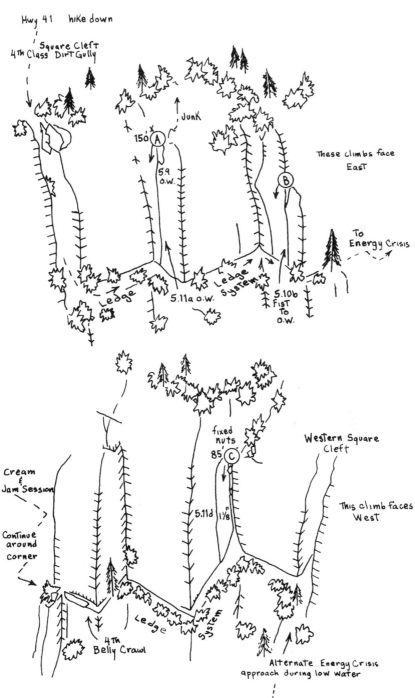

Hwy 41   hike down

Square Cleft
4th Class Dirt Gully

Junk

150' (A)

5.9 o.w.

These climbs face East

(B)

To Energy Crisis

Ledge

Ledge System

5.11a o.w.

5.10b Fist To o.w.

fixed nuts

85' (C)

Western Square Cleft

Cream & Jam Session

This climb faces West

5.11d 1⅛"

Continue around corner

4th Belly Crawl

Ledge System

Alternate Energy Crisis approach during low water

The Rostrum

Park above on Highway 41 at the west end of the long, stone wall west of the Wawona Tunnel. Initially, for all routes, hike down slabs. For the Notch Route, navigate to the rim above the notch. For the other routes, descend the steep, dirt gully that lies immediately west of the Rostrum. The Kauk-ulator starts at the bottom of the gully. The middle of the North Face and Blind Faith can be reached around the corner from The Kauk-ulator via a 5.6 section. To reach the base of the North Face, the drop-off beyond requires four 70-foot rappels. The north face routes may also be approached from below via Highway 140 in times of low water.

NPS photo

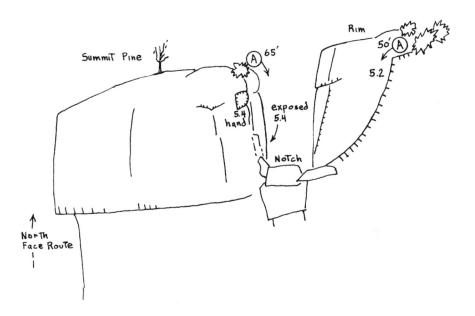

THE ROSTRUM

A　**The Notch Route　5.4　★★**　Pro: A few pieces to 2½ inches. A small climb with a big view. A picnic-type route.

B　**Kauk-ulator　5.11c　★★★**　Pro: ½ to 2½ inches; also include one 3½ inch piece. A stunning straigh-up, slightly overhanging crack. It stays dry in a light rain.

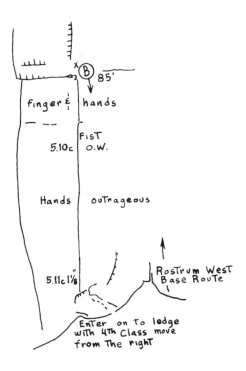

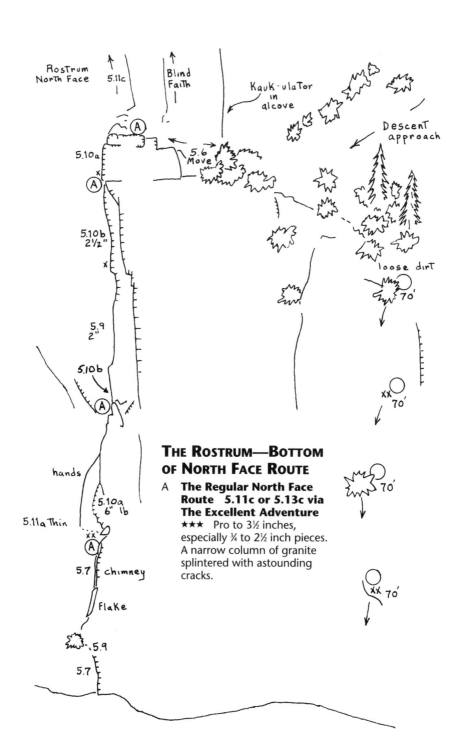

Rostrum
North Face

5.11c

Blind
Faith

Kauk-ulator
in
alcove

Descent
approach

5.10a

5.6
Move

5.10b
2½"

loose dirt

70'

5.9
2"

5.10b

xx
70'

hands

THE ROSTRUM—BOTTOM OF NORTH FACE ROUTE

70'

5.10a
6" lb

5.11a Thin

A **The Regular North Face Route 5.11c or 5.13c via The Excellent Adventure**
★★★ Pro to 3½ inches, especially ¾ to 2½ inch pieces. A narrow column of granite splintered with astounding cracks.

5.7 chimney

Flake

5.9

xx 70'

5.7

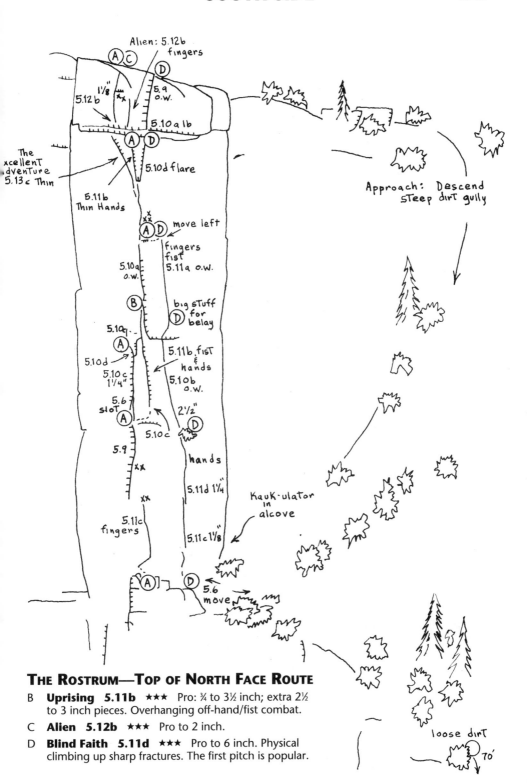

Alien: 5.12b fingers

(A) (C)
(D)
1⅛"
xx
5.12b
5.9 o.w.

5.10a 1b

The xcellenT dvenTure 5.13c Thin

(A) (D)
5.10d flare

5.11b Thin Hands

xx
xx
(A) (D) move left

fingers
fist
5.10a o.w.
5.11a o.w.

(B)
big sTuff for belay
(D)

5.10a
(A)
5.10d
5.10c 1¼"
5.11b fist & hands
5.10b o.w.

5.6 sloT
(A)
5.10c
2½"
(D)

5.9
xx
hands

5.11d 1¼"

xx
Kauk·ulaTor in alcove

5.11c fingers
5.11c 1⅛"

(A) (D) 5.6 move

Approach: Descend sTeep dirT gully

loose dirT
70'

THE ROSTRUM—TOP OF NORTH FACE ROUTE

B **Uprising 5.11b** ★★★ Pro: ¾ to 3½ inch; extra 2½ to 3 inch pieces. Overhanging off-hand/fist combat.

C **Alien 5.12b** ★★★ Pro to 2 inch.

D **Blind Faith 5.11d** ★★★ Pro to 6 inch. Physical climbing up sharp fractures. The first pitch is popular.

ELEPHANT ROCK

1 **Hot Line**
2 **Fatal Mistake**
3 **The Worst Error**
4 **Killer Pillar**

ELEPHANT ROCK—THE WORST ERROR

Park at The Cookie (0.5 miles down from Cascade Fall Bridge on Highway 140) and walk down the road until even with the huge Monster Boulder that lies on the opposite side of the river. This is the best crossing, but can only be done during periods of low water. Once across, hike up the talus.

A **Crash Line 5.11b** ★★ Pro: ¼ to 2 inches, especially ½ to 1¼ inch pieces.

The next three routes follow splitting cracks on a amazing piece of natural architecture: the Worst Error.

B **Hotline 5.12a** ★★★ Pro to 3 inches, including extra 1½ to 2½ inch pieces.

C **Fatal Mistake 5.11a, A1** ★★★ Pro: Small to 3½ inches. Thus far, free attempts on pitch 1 have been unsuccessful. A ploy has been to climb Pink Dream, then arrange two rappels to reach the top of pitch 1. This is an indistinct point, and extra gear should be considered for these rappel/belay stations. Usually, the first rappel is short, and the rope pulled; the second long, and the rope fixed.

D **Pink Dream 5.10a** ★★★ Pro to 3½ inches, including extra 2 to 3 inch pieces; a #11 Hex is useful.

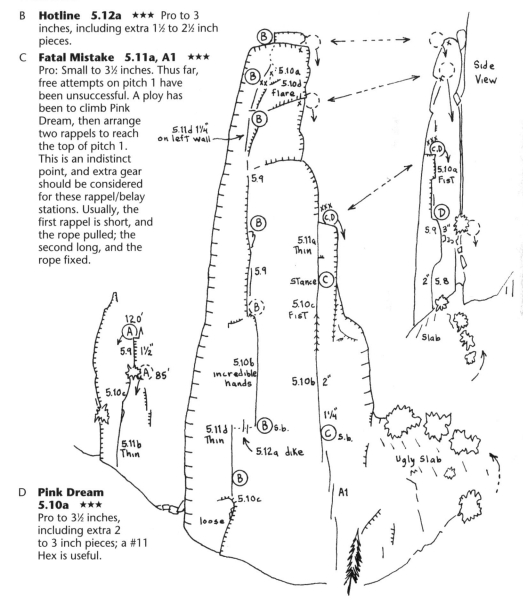

Ed Barry on Fun Terminal, Killer Pillar

Walter J. Flint

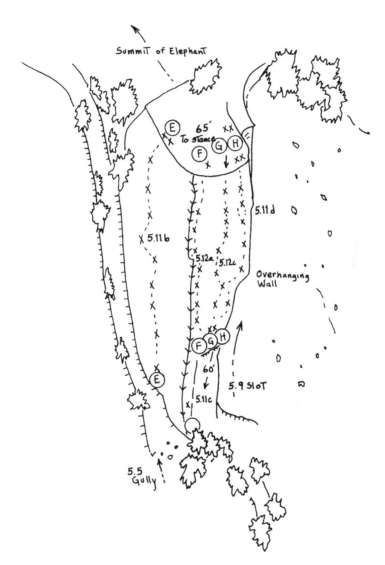

ELEPHANT ROCK—KILLER PILLAR

Park in the banked, gravelled turnout west of the stone wall that is The Rostrum parking. The summit of Elephant Rock can be reached in a few minutes. Careful scouting just beyond will reveal the top of Killer Pillar. Judicious rappelling follows. The wall is overhung and bolts may need to be clipped to avoid being stranded from the belay stance.

E   **The Hundredth Monkey   5.11b**   ★★   Pro: QDs.

F   **Fun Terminal   5.12a**   ★★★   Pro: QDs.

G   **Wicked Gravity   5.12c**   ★★★   Pro: QDs.

H   **Bucket Brigade   5.11d**   ★★★   Pro: QDs.

ACCESS: It's every climber's concern

The Access Fund, a national, non-profit climbers organization, works to keep climbing areas open and to conserve the climbing environment. Need help with closures? land acquisition? legal or land management issues? funding for trails and other projects? starting a local climbers' group? CALL US! Climbers can help preserve access by being committed to Leave No Trace (minimum-impact) practices. Here are some simple guidelines:

- **ASPIRE TO "LEAVE NO TRACE"** especially in environmentally sensitive areas like caves. Chalk can be a significant impact on dark and porous rock—don't use it around historic rock art. Pick up litter, and leave trees and plants intact.

- **DISPOSE OF HUMAN WASTE PROPERLY** Use toilets whenever possible. If toilets are not available, dig a "cat hole" at least six inches deep and 200 feet from any water, trails, campsites, or the base of climbs. *Always pack out toilet paper.* On big wall routes, use a "poop tube" and carry waste up and off with you (the old "bag toss" is now illegal in many areas).

- **USE EXISTING TRAILS** Cutting switchbacks causes erosion. When walking off-trail, tread lightly, especially in the desert where cryptogamic soils (usually a dark crust) take thousands of years to form and are easily damaged. Be aware that "rim ecologies" (the clifftop) are often highly sensitive to disturbance.

- **BE DISCRETE WITH FIXED ANCHORS** *Bolts are controversial and are not a convenience*—don't place 'em unless they are *really* necessary. Camouflage all anchors. Remove unsightly slings from rappel stations (better to use steel chain or welded cold shuts). Bolts sometimes can be used proactively to protect fragile resources—consult with your local land manager.

- **RESPECT THE RULES** and speak up when other climbers don't. Expect restrictions in designated wilderness areas, rock art sites, caves, and to protect wildlife, especially nesting birds of prey. *Power drills are illegal in wilderness and all national parks.*

- **PARK AND CAMP IN DESIGNATED AREAS** Some climbing areas require a permit for overnight camping.

- **MAINTAIN A LOW PROFILE** Leave the boom box and day-glo clothing at home—the less climbers are heard and seen, the better.

- **RESPECT PRIVATE PROPERTY** Be courteous to land owners. Don't climb where you're not wanted.

- **JOIN THE ACCESS FUND** To become a member, make a tax-deductible donation of $25.

The Access Fund

Preserving America's Diverse Climbing Resources
PO Box 17010
Boulder, CO 80308
303.545.6772 • www.accessfund.org